ROBERT PAUL & GREG SMALLEY

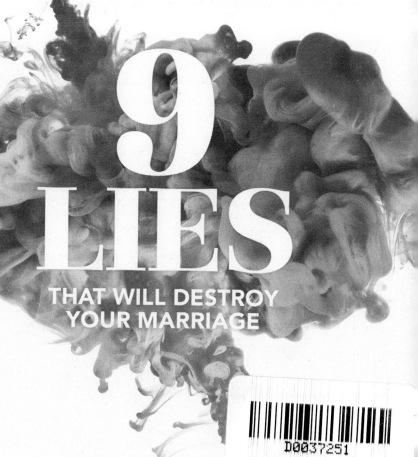

9 LIES

THAT WILL DESTROY YOUR MARRIAGE

**And the Truths That Will
Save It and Set It Free**

TYNDALE HOUSE PUBLISHERS
CAROL STREAM, ILLINOIS

FOCUS ON THE FAMILY®

9 LIES THAT WILL DESTROY YOUR MARRIAGE

CONTENTS

INTRODUCTION:

YOUR JOURNEY TO A BETTER MARRIAGE

Jim and Mary have been married eighteen years but say they now feel more like friends than lovers. "It's like we're roommates, or business partners," says Jim. "Not husband and wife." They want to be closer and go deeper, but they don't know how to get there.

According to their many friends, Marissa and Todd are warm, outgoing, and talkative. But when the two of them try to talk to each other, bombs explode. Even simple discussions about their daily schedules can rapidly veer off track, as unresolved conflicts from a month or a decade earlier resurface and inflame powerful passions.

Roger and Brittany both hoped that marriage would be calmer the second time around. Both left their first marriages because they said their partners subjected them to verbal attacks and abuse. But now, a few years into their marriage, they're too emotionally self-protective to risk sharing openly and honestly with each other.

Beverly and Andrew have been married for thirteen years. Everything seemed perfect for a long time. Now, things are tense, ever since Andrew found out that Beverly, who is fifteen years younger, had an affair with a coworker. She has repeatedly apologized, but a cloud of distance and distrust remains.

These four couples are struggling. Their marriages began with love and hope but have since spiraled downhill.

Now it's a Monday morning, and they're all sitting on big, comfy couches in a meeting room at Focus on the Family's Hope Restored Marriage Intensive in Branson, Missouri. They're hoping for a miracle, and as the leaders of this week's intensive, we're praying that they experience one. We're not miracle workers, but God is.

We've worked with more than seven thousand couples over the last twenty years as retreat leaders and trained therapists. We've reached even more people through our talks and books. All these men and women have provided a type of "marriage lab" for us. And what we keep learning is amazing.

The results have been nothing short of miraculous. Most of the couples who come to us for therapy are in real crisis, many on the brink of divorce. Yet, some of our research indicates that more than 80 percent remain married two years after they let us help them.

We've brought together some of our top marriage insights and tools in the pages that follow. This isn't theory. It's practical wisdom that comes from being able to walk alongside people who struggle to make their marriages stronger. In fact, these are the very tools and strategies our entire team uses in their own lives. If you've been struggling in your marriage, we pray you may find a miracle or two of your own. If not, we know that these insights and tools can make a good marriage even better.

Why We Love Lies About Love

Each couple is unique and faces unique challenges in marriage. But in our decades of working with couples—both in marriages that are healthy and in those that are struggling—we've repeatedly encountered the same major problems happening over and over and over again.

Yes, the individual circumstances of each marriage may be

unique, but the problems we see weakening and destroying marriages are often common and predictable. That's because one of the biggest problems we see is that men and women grow up learning lies about love, lies generally taught by well-meaning people. Then they put these love lies into practice in their marriages, which prevents them from experiencing the wonder and beauty of real love.

Why would people build a marriage on a foundation of attractive but destructive lies instead of building on the solid foundation of God's loving truth? These lies are taught as truth and can be very subtle; sometimes they're even partially true. The problem is, they result in relational strategies that cannot actually work—and we don't realize it. And if we're using fundamentally flawed strategies we've been told are right and will work, what are we left to assume is the problem when these strategies inevitably fail? The people themselves!

Many of these marriage myths have now permeated our culture, filtering down even into our churches and our dating and marriage rituals. Sadly, we allow these insidious ideas to burrow deep down in the foundations of our marriages and fatally weaken the whole structure.

In this book we will be exploring the biggest lies we've seen at work in people's relationships. We think of them as big, ugly, hungry termites designed to devour and destroy the foundations of love and marriage.

For example, chapter 2 will shine a light on the "1 + 1 = 1" lie. This particular myth may seem attractive when heard in just the right circumstances—for example, when Tom Cruise looks passionately at Renée Zellweger in the movie *Jerry Maguire* and declares, "You complete me." Or when Elvis Presley belts out the chorus of his 1956 hit "I Want You, I Need You, I Love You."

The "1 + 1 = 1" lie sounds romantic, like something you might see in a greeting card or love note. But we've talked to many spouses who started off wanting to generously provide the key ingredients to fulfill and complete their incomplete partners. Yet after years of genuine effort, they don't know why they appear to be failing and their spouses still feel unfulfilled.

We've seen the sad legacy of this attractive but destructive lie in hundreds of couples unknowingly caught in the webs of codependency—the belief held by many spouses that they must look to their partners to find their true happiness, sense of self-worth, and identity.

In chapter 9 we'll explore the popular lie that says fights between marriage partners are natural and unavoidable, but that everything will be okay if everyone just remembers to fight fair and make up afterward. We have personally seen the destructive impact of this lie in hundreds of couples who can't settle conflicts without going ballistic and attacking or tearing each other down, leaving both partners emotionally (and sometimes physically) wounded and scarred.

As we show you the destructive power of these major marriage lies in people's lives, we will point toward stronger foundations to build on, foundations based on our Creator's will and design for marriage.

Because the lies we've loved and lived with all our lives don't suddenly disappear overnight once we see the light, we'll also lead you through some of the techniques and tools we've used ourselves and with the many couples we've counseled. If you want a marriage that's stronger, more loving, and more resilient, these time-tested tools will help you make steady progress.

Consider the Source

We've worked with people of all religions and creeds, but most of our work is with Christian couples, and when we work with believers, we talk about the spiritual forces and powers that are at play in our lives. That same Christian view will also be our vantage point for this book.

As you will see, our faith is more than a collection of Bible verses or dos and don'ts. We believe in a living relationship with Christ, the One who rose from the dead and is active in real ways in our lives.

But God is not the only spiritual force in our cosmos. His Enemy, the devil, is at work as well. We see his evil imprint all over the lies we'll explore here. After all, he is the author of lies.

So why would the devil spend his time trying to destroy marriages? Because marriage is one of God's greatest and most glorious gifts. As we will see, marriage is about much more than just two people and their personal happiness. There are larger legacies at stake, and the devil wants to tear apart as many marriages as possible.

We see his impact when men and women believe his lies and try to make them work in their marriages. We also see his power when he succeeds in turning men and women against each other.

We know that some people think it's silly or medievally old-fashioned to talk of the devil impacting marriages for the worse. But that's just the way the devil likes us to remain: blind to all his varied schemes.

We have seen the devil and his lies create hatred where there should be love, distance and division where there should be oneness and unity, and family separation and generational pain where there should be strong family legacies continuing generation after generation.

Men and women need to realize there are supernatural forces at work in our lives and marriages. We shouldn't be surprised that the evil force wants to cause chaos and distrust in our relationships. The warnings Peter gave apply to couples: "Be sober-minded;

be watchful. Your adversary the devil prowls around like a roaring lion, seeking someone to devour" (1 Peter 5:8).

Paul also warned against the devil's schemes:

> Finally, be strong in the Lord and in the strength of his might. Put on the whole armor of God, that you may be able to stand against the schemes of the devil. For we do not wrestle against flesh and blood, but against the rulers, against the authorities, against the cosmic powers over this present darkness, against the spiritual forces of evil in the heavenly places. Therefore take up the whole armor of God, that you may be able to withstand in the evil day, and having done all, to stand firm.
>
> EPHESIANS 6:10-13

The devil is real, and he is out to destroy you and ruin your marriage. We're not saying this so you can mistreat and abuse your partner then turn around and blame it on the devil. We are simply warning you that as we explore the lies that destroy marriages, don't forget to guard yourself and your marriage from the author of these lies.

Just remember: *My partner isn't my enemy, but the devil is.*

Twin Brothers of Different Mothers?

No matter what kind of marriage you have, we want to invite you to join us on a journey toward a better marriage based on God's design.

If your marriage is good but could be better, we want to help you make it great.

If your marriage is in crisis, and you feel everything will fall apart unless you get emergency care, we want to hold your hand and help you get a clear understanding of your situation and what you can do.

But before we launch our journey to a better marriage, please let us introduce ourselves to you.

Each of us has known of the other's work for decades, and the two of us have worked together for years, having cofounded Focus on the Family's Hope Restored Marriage Intensive program. Now we have the chance to collaborate more closely again, and we couldn't be more excited.

We're 100 percent committed to helping couples improve their marriages. We've seen broken marriages healed and restored. We've seen good marriages become great marriages. We've seen marriages that neither partner appreciated become transformed into marriages both partners absolutely love.

Both of us grew up in families known for pioneering approaches to help people enjoy deeper and happier marriages. Today, both of us choose to continue in "the family business." For us, it's not something we inherited or simply a career path we chose. It's our life's work, our sacred calling, our mission, our ministry, our passion.

Greg's Story

My dad, Gary Smalley, may have been the world's most famous Christian marriage counselor. Today all three of Gary and Norma's children remain involved in this vital work. For my part, I serve as the vice president of Marriage at Focus.

You may have seen Gary during some of his many TV appearances on popular programs including *The Oprah Winfrey Show* and *Fox & Friends*. Or perhaps you heard him speak to millions of men at Promise Keepers rallies, attended one of his marriage conferences, heard one of his fifty Focus on the Family broadcasts, read one of his sixty books (they've sold more than five million copies), or watched one of his marriage videos (more than nine million sold).

It was fun having a famous dad who counseled and coached so many people, including John Tesh and Connie Sellecca, and Frank and Kathie Lee Gifford. Even better, he was the same man at home with us as he was up on stage. He was a man of prayer and Bible study who spent his life honoring his wife and family.

Whenever he did something foolish—as all of us do—he was humble enough to admit he had made a mistake. He constantly sought to grow and learn, both as a dad and follower of Christ. He was one expert who was never too proud to tell people that he had messed up as a husband and father.

"I haven't arrived yet," he would often say. "I'll arrive when I get to heaven."

Dad was authentic and transparent, and this helped his three children embrace his deep faith in Christ to make it our own. He saw the importance of a good relationship with his children, telling me once that having a child was like making a best friend. I can honestly say that he was one of my best friends.

He also had a great sense of humor, which came in handy for me the time he woke up from a nap to find that my brother, Michael, and I had clasped the dog's electric bark collar around his neck. He didn't get mad when we made loud barking sounds and the collar zapped him.

Dad went to heaven in 2016. I was by his side when he died, me having just spoken at a big marriage conference. There are times when I'm counseling couples, or speaking about marriage at conferences, or writing a book like this one, and I feel like I'm following in his footsteps. That makes me happy.

Bob's Story

Like Greg, I grew up in a family of popular, best-selling marriage gurus. And like Greg, I inherited their love of counseling, eventually deciding to follow in their footsteps by working as a marriage counselor, author, lecturer, and college professor.

But unlike Greg, I grew up in a broken home. My parents

divorced when I was only a year old. My mom remarried when I was three and my dad remarried when I was five. But I always felt loved by all four adults in my life.

Another important difference was that I didn't grow up in a Christian home. My dad and stepmom's underlying philosophy of life was more "New Agey" than Christian. I would not become a follower of Jesus until the day before my wedding, at twenty-three (and that's a story in itself!). Coming to faith in Christ changed my whole paradigm not only for life but also for helping couples who struggle in marriage.

I came to idolize my father, Jordan, and was inspired by my stepmother, Margie. I watched them pioneer ideas and techniques in marriage and relational counseling. They coauthored the best-selling marriage book *Do I Have to Give Up Me to Be Loved by You?*, which has sold more than a million copies and been translated into ten languages. They promoted their books on TV shows such as *The Oprah Winfrey Show* and *The Phil Donahue Show*.

With fame and a private practice in West Los Angeles came opportunities to work with celebrities. My stepmom even coached one famous actress so she could play a convincing therapist in a famous, award-winning movie.

Another memory of my youth: The day after actress and *Playboy* Playmate Pamela Anderson appeared on *The Tonight Show with Jay Leno* and raved to Jay about how Margie had helped her, media film crews showed up at our house clamoring to interview my stepmother for the next news broadcast.

For me, the most exciting opportunity was the five years I had the privilege to work alongside my stepmom, helping her Los Angeles–based company, Inner Bonding Educational Technologies, facilitate dozens of five-day group therapy intensives throughout the country. I truly had the opportunity to learn from one of the best.

While other therapists were sitting alone figuring out their practice, I was sitting side by side with a master, doing therapy with her and learning all I could about leading group therapy intensives. Seeing my stepmom help people discover and address their problems made me fall in love with this kind of intensive, valuable counseling work, and I'm grateful I've spent my life doing it.

Counselors' Confessions

Our families of origin couldn't be more different, but they introduced both of us to the calling we would follow all our lives: helping men and women build better marriages.

So our professional partnership is based on the same things that provide a solid foundation for good marriages: love for each other, mutual respect, a desire to learn from and serve each other, and a commitment to truth and honesty. That commitment to truth and honesty means we must confess something to you, dear reader: If you bought this book based on the assumption that our track records as therapists would enable us to have perfect marriages and families, you should probably stop reading now.

Each of us is a broken, selfish man who has struggled with the same issues you face. Remember the love lies? We've believed them all, at least in part, and tried them out before we found them lacking. Like other married men and women around the world, we're still constantly working on this important relationship.

We thank God that each of us has been married for a long time: Greg for more than twenty-eight years and Bob for more than thirty-nine. Both of us confess that there were times when it seemed our marriages would not survive. But we have worked to make our marriages better day after day, year after year, decade after decade. We hope the same for you.

Let the Journey Begin

God designed marriage as an amazing gift for men and women, their families, and our world. He wants us to experience this gift in all its richness.

The couples you met at the beginning of this chapter aren't experiencing this gift to its fullest. Perhaps you feel the same way.

But you can make your marriage better if you want to. If your marriage is in crisis, you can help it not only survive but thrive. We've seen many broken and imperfect marriages transformed. If your marriage is great and you want it to grow to be even greater, you can take it to a new level. We've seen men and women weave strong, lasting relationships overflowing with love, beauty, and grace.

Our goal in this book is to live out the goal in Scripture: "Let marriage be held in honor among all" (Hebrews 13:4).

We have a vision for you: We want you to enjoy a healthy, happy, growing marriage that you and your partner both love. But that's not the end. It's just the beginning of this vision, a vision that your great marriage will become contagious. Wouldn't it be amazing if more couples had marriages that were so exciting and fulfilling that everyone around them wanted what they had? And what if some of those couples not only took care of their own marriages but also invested time and energy in helping other people who want to have a healthy marriage? What a powerful way to steward this amazing gift God has given us—a gift that many of us have messed up. But we have a vision that thousands of men and women enjoying these healthy and contagious relationships will grow into a marriage movement that helps men and women realize this beauty for themselves.

May God bless you on your journey to a better marriage. Let's start the journey by taking a look at something many people don't really understand: God's design for a healthy marriage.

LOVE LIE #1:

AND THEY LIVED HAPPILY EVER AFTER

Katie and Zach were the kind of cute, contented couple that people loved to be around. "They look so happy together," said friends, family members, and church members who knew them. Each was considered attractive and a good catch as a potential mate. Both were cheerful, with glass-half-full attitudes. Even when at rest, their lips formed nice smiles, not frowns. A few of their friends jokingly referred to them as Ken and Barbie because they were as blond and sculpted as the popular dolls.

Their romance had a fairy-tale quality to it. Introduced to each other by friends who promised, "You will be perfect for each other," they actually were, quickly falling in love and making plans for their big wedding. And in the months before their marriage, they spent most evenings going out to dinner and seeing movies. When they saw Disney's *The Lion King*, they both cried as Simba triumphed over his archrival, Scar.

Their love of film—particularly Disney movies and romantic comedies with happy endings—led them to add this line to their marriage ceremony: "And they lived happily ever after!"

It's Complicated!

For years Katie and Zach were happy. They loved each other, enjoyed the same things, and built a loving home and family together. The front yard of their suburban home even had a picket fence! (The paint was taupe, though, not white.)

"We went into marriage expecting we would be happy," Zach offered, when he and Katie first came to us. "Why get married if you don't think you would be happy?"

But over time, alien elements of unhappiness invaded their love nest. The problems started soon after the birth of their first child, an overactive boy.

"Everybody told us we'd be tired," Katie said, "but we had no idea *how* tired."

Strange feelings began to cloud their relationship. They disagreed over whose turn it was to do the 4 a.m. feeding, and they found themselves disappointed to experience these petty arguments.

"We truly love our precious baby boy but feel guilty about not being 'good enough' parents," Zach confessed. "We even feel guilty about feeling guilty!"

There was no more time for dining out, going to movies, or even talking.

After two weeks of paid paternity leave, Zach couldn't wait to return to the people and predictability at his work. Over the following weeks, Katie grew resentful that Zach now helped her less, and Zach became frustrated.

"I don't get it," Zach said. "We need my income now more than ever."

Unhappily Seeking Happiness

In time, a pattern developed. After problems arose, things would then calm down again and life would return to normal. But each new normal seemed a few steps below their original ideals. A simmering discontent grew between them.

"We were so young and innocent when we said we would live happily ever after," Katie said. "But right now, nobody's happy!"

Their scenario is far from unusual. Happy endings happen frequently in fairy tales and romantic movies, but real life turns out to be a bit more complicated and messy.

Zach and Katie embraced a popular version of the "Happily Ever After" lie. They had come to believe:

- A good marriage is like a big greenhouse that grows happiness.
- If happiness is fading, so is the marriage.
- If happiness is gone, so is the marriage.

Unfortunately, they've set themselves on a path that leads in a downward spiral. When happiness is seen as a major purpose for getting married, lack of happiness can lead to disappointment, frustration, and even comparison to other marriages perceived to be happier than theirs.

Now, as the distance between Katie and Zach has grown, feelings of happiness are increasingly rare, replaced by feelings of discouragement and being cheated. They want to work and make things better, but both question whether it would require too much investment and whether it would be worth it.

We've seen this story before. The people and the details change, but the impact of the "Happily Ever After" lie remains. Unmet expectations for continued happiness in marriage are actually one of the greatest causes of marital disappointment.

A Reasonable Pursuit, a Problematic Goal

Katie and Zach are facing a problem, and in some ways, it's commonly an American problem. Understandably, we Americans believe in happiness and aggressively seek it out. Many of us even consider it a "right," based on our recognition of its mention in our Declaration of Independence: "We hold these truths to be self-evident, that all men are created equal, that they are endowed by their Creator with certain unalienable Rights, that among these are Life, Liberty and the pursuit of Happiness."

But look carefully. The Declaration defends our right to *pursue* happiness, but does that statement mean to suggest that nothing is more important?

For many people, the pursuit of happiness becomes the primary purpose of both life and marriage. Since they believe they will be happier with someone, they want to team up with a partner in order to make each other *supremely* happy. But unfortunately, once happiness becomes the main goal of marriage, all the normal ups and downs and challenges of life can pose serious dangers to the relationship. And in some cases, marital unhappiness becomes a potential justification for emotional distance, affairs, or divorce.

When things go south in our marriages, when they don't live up to our hopes and expectations, or when there are periods of dissatisfaction, the commitment to stay together becomes strained, and people often say things like:

"This isn't what I had in mind."

"I've fallen out of love with my partner."

"I didn't sign up for this."

"There's something wrong with my spouse."

"We've grown apart."

"This is just too hard and painful."

"I don't want to do this anymore."

Or, as Katie often said, "Sometimes I don't even remember why we married each other."

Seeing God's Higher Purposes for Your Marriage

Let's stop for a minute, take a deep breath, and look at Katie and Zach's particular scenario. Is it possible that they've bought into a flawed picture about what constitutes happiness? Are they navigating toward a fairy-tale destination that's illusory rather than attempting to identify and align with the truth of God's intent?

God wants men and women to be really happy in marriage. That's part of why He created it. As the Lord declares throughout Scripture, He loves us and wants us to be full of joy. But that's not the whole story. Marital happiness is only one aspect of God's much bigger picture for this important relationship.

Jesus said, "I have come that they may have life, and have it to the full" (John 10:10, NIV). The word *full* here means over and above, more than enough. God wants us to experience not only the fullness of joy in Him, but also the fullness of *life* through gifts of His such as marriage.

Somewhere along the way we've become confused about how to experience life fully. Katie and Zach believed happiness was their primary purpose in life. But is happiness the only meaningful aspect of life? How about things like relationships, family, caring, compassion, creativity, creating, learning, growing, freedom, commitment, effort, devotion, hope, vision, sacrifice, making a difference, teamwork, and on and on? As important as happiness is, we struggle to imagine that it's more important than the rest of these.

In fact, we are confident that God wants us all to be personally blessed. However, His purposes for us individually, and His purposes for us in the world, are much bigger than just our personal blessings.

We have good news for Katie and Zach and the many other people who are having problems experiencing the marital happiness they've dreamed of. When God created marriage, He meant the blessings to extend beyond just Zach and Katie, beyond just you and me. He is at work on a larger plan, and it's clear He wants us to be a part of it with Him: God sees marriage as a powerful relationship that can help redeem the world and build His Kingdom.

Don't get us wrong. We like happiness. We're not fundamentalist killjoys promoting the benefits of pain and suffering. Rather, we're enthusiastic believers in the idea that begins the Westminster Shorter Catechism:

Q. What is the chief end of man?
A. Man's chief end is to glorify God, and to enjoy him forever.

We are incredibly pro-happiness. Happiness is a good thing, and marriage often makes people happier. But there's so much more to marriage than just the feelings of two people. God created marriage for your good, but He also has purposes that are far more meaningful and far-reaching.

Let's take a look at some of God's higher purposes for your marriage.

Your Partner in the Journey of Life

Many of you probably remember studying the famous Lewis and Clark Expedition, commissioned by President Thomas Jefferson, that set out to map the previously uncharted territory west of the Mississippi River to the Pacific Ocean. Where would Meriwether Lewis have been without his fellow explorer, William Clark? It's likely that if either of these men had tried to cross the continent alone, neither would have survived or achieved their amazing exploits.

The trip included circumstances that were sometimes awe-inspiring, sometimes miraculous, sometimes difficult, and sometimes life-threatening. Along the way they discovered things that had never been known or recorded before. Because they worked together and helped each other out, they were successful on a journey that covered more than 7,500 miles over two and a half years.

We want you to think about Lewis and Clark as you consider the purpose of marriage. You and your spouse may not be mapping the American wilderness, but you are creating your own maps together as you walk together in the journey of life. As a married couple you are now commissioned by God to go on a sacred journey with Him *and* your spouse. The marital expedition has potential personal, community, and Kingdom purposes. We want to help you embrace a vision of some of the ways your marriage can benefit both you and the world so you don't miss all God wants to show you.

When we work with couples like Zach and Katie, we encourage them to try and embrace a paradigm shift in the way they look at each other and the state of their marriages. They started out believing that they would help each other live happily ever after. Now they're running into problems with that model, but that doesn't mean their marriage is fatally endangered. It just means they were trying to arrive at the wrong destination.

Instead of seeing your partner as the primary source of your happiness in marriage, we want you to take a fresh look and see your partner as something better—something more! On one level, your spouse is designed to be your journeying partner, walking alongside you and supporting you as you confront the issues and challenges you will face in life.

Have you ever experienced a success or victory but lacked someone to share your joy? Or have you ever experienced a humiliating defeat but lacked someone to help you carry the emotional burden? These are the *supportive roles* you and your partner can serve for each other. However, as great as that can be, there's even more beyond your personal journey. Together with your journeying partner you can experience an even deeper sense of purpose that is possible when you join together with God, focused on His plan.

Have you ever worked as part of a team that accomplished something special? Generally, the hard work required only adds to the value of what was achieved. Or have you pulled together with others in valiant effort, only to come up a little short? Perhaps rather than seeing that experience as a failure, you all learned important lessons together. Everyone involved grew as a result, increasing the likelihood of future success.

As two of God's intentionally designed children, your lives were created on purpose, with purpose. Once married, your spouse is also meant to be your life partner, working together with you to create and build beautiful and significant things. These relational activities reflect some of the *creative roles* you and your spouse can have together in marriage.

I (Greg) have some good friends, Brian and Kari, who made great money investing in commercial real estate in New York City. They were living very comfortably and enjoying all the city had to offer. And then one day they started wondering if this was going to be their life—eating out every night at the best restaurants, orchestra row seats on Broadway, Fifth Avenue shopping, exclusive parties, and so on.

But God began tugging at their hearts. One day while they were walking around Central Park, they talked about how they might use their marriage to serve others. They didn't have a clear vision but had a peace that they were supposed to do something more with the financial blessings they'd been given. As their hearts joined around a common call, they felt united and supported.

That Sunday, as they were listening to a sermon about serving God, the visiting preacher flashed a verse on the screen that caused them both to well up with tears: "To you [God] the helpless commits himself; you have been the helper of the fatherless" (Psalm 10:14). Instantly they knew they were being called to care for the fatherless—orphans. But where? How?

Several weeks later, Brian had a meeting with a gentleman who was seeking an investor for a business idea in Beijing, China. As Brian listened to the man's pitch, he suddenly had a clear vision: He could use the profits from this business in China to fund an orphanage. Kari's spirit was moved by the idea, and she felt complete confirmation. So Brian and Kari left the comforts of New York City and headed to China with their three young daughters in tow.

Soon after getting the factory up and running, Kari discovered a need for foster care for medically needy children in Chinese orphanages. After months of red tape and hard work, Brian and Kari opened their first medical foster-care home outside of Beijing. Over the years, they've cared for hundreds of orphans and have seen more than 360 children get adopted worldwide—many to become members of Christian families. In service to the Lord, together they *created* something amazing and beautiful.

Erin and I are so grateful that God gave Brian and Kari a vision of how they could use their marriage to invest in others. Had it not been for their foster-care homes, a newborn baby girl left on their doorstep would not have survived the night. Annie, as they named her, would have never made the 6,300-mile flight to America, where she became our youngest daughter. The point of this story is not that in order to become journeying partners you must leave everything and become missionaries. But because Brian and Kari joined in their calling as a married couple to be the helper of the fatherless and journey together as friends and followers of Christ, they meaningfully contributed to our journey to complete our family and help build our Christ-honoring family legacy.

Your Intimate Friend

One of the main reasons God created marriage was so you could experience deep, meaningful friendship with your primary journeying partner. Your marriage is a vehicle to share moments of joy, passion, and pleasure that could seem empty if you were alone. This gift is also a vehicle to share moments of sadness and sorrow that might crush you if you faced them alone. Marriage provides the ideal stimulus for personal growth as you become more fully the man or woman God created you to be. Simply put, you and your spouse have an opportunity to experience the deepest form of friendship and love there is. You have an opportunity to journey through life with a person who is united with you in love *and* purpose.

In addition, marriage can be a creative, positive agent of hope and change for a world desperately in need. How many people in your circles right now need to see examples of marriages that actually work, personally and relationally? Marriages where couples face normal challenges and difficulties, but they face them together as teammates? They overcome together, and together they learn and grow.

We're also talking about marriages that understand God's activity in this world and intentionally join in to make a difference in the world and in those around them. These are the marriages that demonstrate what is really possible with God—in part, by being deeply satisfying and full of joy, but also being connected to a greater purpose. We see this as *intimate friendship* at its best.

Now that's something to be happy about, and studies show that working on building a deeper friendship with your spouse can be one of life's greatest sources of happiness. And this growing friendship can transform your marriage into one of deep satisfaction and meaningful purpose, even when encountering the challenges that precede every accomplishment and every victory. In real life the obstacles themselves become important elements in the story, just like every inspirational story you've ever heard. Real people who are facing and overcoming real problems with patience and love, who become great friends in the process, are the elements of any real love story.

When we shift our ultimate goal from happiness to having a satisfying intimate friendship filled with meaning and purpose, our relationship foundation fundamentally changes. The result becomes a relationship that truly inspires others to want what you have.

When those newly inspired couples then take those same steps to transform their marriages, they now become a source of inspiration to others, too. As more and more couples join in, we all begin to show the world what's possible in marriage with Christ, and over time we restore marriage to its rightful place of honor (see Hebrews 13:4). This may sound at first like a pipe dream, but this is actually what we have been doing now for more than twenty years. Not just with us personally, but with thousands of other couples too.

More than You and Me

When we work with couples like Katie and Zach, we want to help them experience more happiness in marriage. We also want to challenge them to cast a bigger vision for their life together based on God's design.

Here are four ways God uses marriage to help us to look beyond ourselves and our own happiness.

1. Marriage Transforms Lives

Martin Luther called marriage a school for character. Your marriage has the potential of continually transforming you, your partner, and your children, so that all of you daily grow closer to becoming the people God created you to be.

Zach and Katie's emphasis on personal happiness has somewhat short-circuited this higher purpose. Because engaging in deep conversations may create differences or tensions, they have shied away from such talks, preferring to keep things light and superficial. Unfortunately, this means they often miss out on their potential to partner with each other in their mutual redemption, healing, and growth. Yet marriage can help us become all we were created to be if we let it do so.

2. Marriage Is Proof of God's Love

God is love, but not everyone sees or believes that. Some people are skeptical because they see God's followers often acting in non-loving ways. Other people don't even believe real love exists in our world because they don't see it practiced.

You and your spouse have an opportunity to turn the tables on this despair and show the world that true, faithful, devoted love really exists outside of fairy tales and Disney movies. Simply by loving each other and letting that love be seen by others wherever you go, the two of you can serve as powerful ambassadors for God's love.

3. Marriage Is a Way to Share Love with Your Neighbors

Remember when the rich young man asked Jesus what the main commandment was? Jesus told him there were actually *two* main commandments: "You shall love the Lord your God with all your heart and with all your soul and with all your mind. This is the great and first commandment. And a second is like it: You shall love your neighbor as yourself. On these two commandments depend all the Law and the Prophets" (Matthew 22:37-40).

Families are one of God's favorite ways of spreading His love and grace around in a world that needs it. Think about it: Your love has the potential of revealing God's love to others and to the world.

Zach and Katie's friendship now permeates a loving household. With open hearts and open arms, their house becomes a home. New opportunities abound to practice hospitality and share that love with people outside, and the mat on the front doorstep simply says, "Welcome."

They may not *yet* be as happy as they might like to be, or as happy as they're likely to become. But happiness frequently finds us along the way when we truly embrace and engage our intimate friendship journey through marriage.

As Zach and Katie continue to develop this friendship, they have ongoing opportunity to serve as both models and mentors to other couples who are floundering, helping those couples embrace their own journeys.

Their marriage now more fully reveals God's love to all the men and women they meet. As they step out, let others know them, and share that love, they positively impact their neighborhood, church, and community. It creates a powerful cultural impact.

4. Marriage Becomes a Living Legacy

Have you ever noticed how many married couples have children? What a privilege it is to cocreate a whole new life and prepare this person to make the world a better place. The legacy of your children will outlast your own marriage and your life, and so this legacy is worth your investment. Although parenting and raising children is not the focus of this book, it's a central piece of God's design for marriage.

However, even beyond our children, couples who are living as intimate friends connected together with God and His purposes demonstrate what God can do in and through marriage. We live in a culture that questions whether a good, godly marriage is even possible or relevant in the world today. We hear young people ask, "Why would I want to get married when I don't know anyone married any length of time who's happy?"

We wholeheartedly believe that great marriages are not only possible but are actually the cornerstone of God's plan for families, communities, and the world. Together we can show the world what *is* possible with God and those submitted to His purpose. We can create marriages that are deeply satisfying and filled with rich meaning and purpose.

Then, as our successful marriages are seen by others, they become an inspiration. As those couples then create their own enjoyable and meaningful journeys together, our marriages have created a powerful, positive legacy that can be passed on from generation to generation.

An Elusive Goal

Zach and Katie have been unhappy—there's no denying that. But even though happiness is important, Zach and Katie have over-rated and overemphasized it. God's primary purpose in marriage is not merely to grow their personal happiness.

Think about it: Happiness can be elusive at times, and it actually seems to be most elusive when we seek it most desperately. Ultimately, our happiness is subject to the many variables and circumstances in life. Everything from bad weather to hunger can heavily impact our moment-to-moment feelings.

That's why it's dangerous to evaluate the success and quality of a marriage by a simple happiness quotient. The things you and

I do to be happier may not be directly tied to the happiness we experience at any particular time.

So rather than focusing on happiness, we want to help you learn how you can experience joy in your marriage journey, even amidst difficulties. Let's see how that can work.

Self-Assessment: What's the Purpose of Marriage?

All married people seek to be happy, but not all marriages achieve this goal. Answer the questions and respond to the statements below to evaluate your feelings.

1. Why did you get married? What is your marriage primarily about?

   Zach and Katie made happiness a priority. Is that why you got married? Reflect on your decision to marry and the reasons you chose this mode of living.

2. I don't look to my spouse to be my source of happiness, but rather as my journeying partner who I can count on to be with me in good times and also through life's challenges.

1	2	3	4	5	6	7
Never		Rarely		Sometimes		Always

3. My spouse and I are clear about, and actively pursuing, the fulfillment of the larger calling and purposes of our marriage, the impact of which reach beyond just us.

1	2	3	4	5	6	7
Never		Rarely		Sometimes		Always

4. Beyond being lovers, our marriage is characterized by being a deep and personal friendship.

1	2	3	4	5	6	7
Never		Rarely		Sometimes	Always	

Exercises for Friends on the Marriage Journey

Horizontal Communication: Rekindling the Lost Art of Conversation

Once upon a time, Jenni and I (Bob), like Katie and Zach, couldn't wait to see each other and talk to each other. Throughout our early life together we were enthralled and infatuated by getting to know each other. We went out to dinner, went to the beach to watch sunsets, went on walks together, enthusiastically asking each other questions and telling each other our life stories.

But as time went on, our conversations became increasingly dominated by the many frustrations and disappointments we encountered. Our "talks" went from enjoying getting to know each other to trying to resolve conflicts. Sadly, growing our friendship became a distant memory.

Unfortunately, we know we're not alone in this. Many people struggle to find either the time or the interest to sit down and have an open-ended conversation with their spouses. That's too bad, because conversation motivated by a desire to know each other waters relationships and nourishes love. It's hard to grow love and friendship without good conversation.

Friendship-building conversation is under assault today by the pace of life, addictive digital devices, and 24/7 media and entertainment options. How often have you seen this picture? Two people sit together having dinner in a restaurant, but they don't talk to each other, focusing instead on their phones.

We're on a crusade to grow great, inspiring marriages based

on real, intimate friendship. Toward that end, we're going to be exploring all kinds of conversations during our journey together in this book. But let's begin with the basics.

When we encounter couples like Zach and Katie, we prescribe a precise procedure to cure their lack of communication: regular conversations full of curiosity, just like the kinds of conversations that build all great friendships and romances. During a typical day, husbands and wives have all kinds of conversations, from simple logistical check-ins (Who's going to pick up some milk on the way home?) to the deepest kinds of heart-to-heart talks (So do we think I should explore this new career opportunity with greater responsibility and greater income?).

We want you to start conversations with a different goal: to build friendship though curiosity. Your goal here is not to deal with family logistics or fix a relational problem. Think of your goal as getting reacquainted with someone you've lost contact with over the years by kindling curiosity. The underlying excitement of infatuation and romance is the fascination of getting to know someone interesting. Treat yourself to the joy of infatuation and romance by allowing yourself to rediscover and cultivate your fascination and interest in your spouse.

Here are some of our recommended conversation starters:

- How was your day? (Warning: Some couples often ask this question but don't wait to hear the answer. Ask this and other questions only if you are really interested to hear what the other person has to say.)
- What's the most interesting experience you had in the last week?
- What is something you're looking forward to?
- What is something you're dreading?

- Where were you and what were you doing on this date ten years ago? Twenty years ago?
- If your life were a big book, what chapter would you say you are in right now?
- If you could ask God to completely eradicate one problem in this world, what would it be?
- Who would you say are the friends you most enjoy being with and talking to?
- Has someone recently disappointed or offended you?
- What are two things that I still don't know about you?
- What is one thing you appreciate about our relationship?
- If you were to die tomorrow, what would be the one thing you've felt best about accomplishing in life? What is the one thing that has been your biggest waste of time?
- What are you feeling most grateful for today?

Horizontal Affirmation: Appreciating Your Partner
When you ask your partner a curiosity question, we want you to do two things:

1. Listen instead of talking. (You are allowed to ask clarifying questions, but don't talk. It's not about you!)
2. Take good notes, because you can use some of the information you learn in our next recommended tool.

Katie and Zach quit talking long ago. About the same time, they also stopped appreciating each other, as their annoyances with each other grew.

To turn this process around, we want you to develop a "Cherish List," itemizing twenty to thirty items that you appreciate and love about your partner. What qualities of character or behaviors do you most appreciate? What about your partner makes you smile or laugh?

We both regularly practice this partner appreciation exercise with our wives. Here are a few of the items we have articulated to let them know specifically what we appreciate about them, followed by a few of their items about us.

What Bob most appreciates about Jenni:
- She's artistic and creative. She makes everything around her more beautiful. She's also an incredibly creative problem solver.
- She's loyal. (She calls it "dysfunctionally loyal.") Her commitment to God, me, and our family is without exception. Without this, among other things, we'd have never made it!
- She's an outside-the-box thinker. Her perspective is so different that at times it seems odd. But because she sees the world differently than anyone else I know, I've been able to see some things I never would have otherwise.

What Jenni most appreciates about Bob:
- His sense of humor. He loves to make others laugh, especially me, even though the jokes are sometimes really dumb!
- His passion for life and hunger to learn. He approaches life with real passion and loves to help others find their own.
- His commitment to God and family. He's never given up on God. Even when times were tough and uncertain, he has yielded to the Lord.

What Greg most appreciates about Erin:
- She's highly relational. She loves being with people and relating to them, especially other women.
- She's diligent: She likes to accomplish a lot in each day.
- She's compassionate: She loves to help others when they are hurting both physically and emotionally. That's why she became a nurse and now works as a counselor.

What Erin most appreciates about Greg:
- He has a great sense of humor and he's a lot of fun to be around.
- He is a hard worker and a great provider for our family.
- He has a sensitive heart. He is gentle and kind with me and our children.

Here are some words and phrases you might use to help you articulate precisely what your partner means to you:

humble	generous
happy	creative
courageous	full of integrity
funny	intelligent
self-confident	sensitive
loyal	curious
caring	responsible
determined	fun loving

When you praise your spouse, be precise about what you appreciate so you can avoid two major problems:

1. When you are vague or overly general ("You are awesome"), your partner has no idea about the specific things you appreciate most.

2. When you focus on external characteristics of attractiveness ("You are incredibly hot!"), your partner may conclude that the attraction is all physical and has nothing to do with other characteristics, so remember to focus primarily on interior qualities and personality traits.

Vertical Communication: Couples That Pray Together Stay Together
It's important for Zach and Katie to communicate with each other and appreciate each other, but there's a third form of communication couples need to keep their love growing deeper: communication with God.

Praying together as a couple is more than a reassuring ritual. It's a way to connect your lives to your Creator and show that, ultimately, the two of you depend on Him for your sustenance—not each other.

Prayer can help the two of you in profound ways. First, it's a way to lay your anxieties and issues before God rather than continually beating each other up with them. Paul's advice on prayer is particularly helpful for couples facing stress: "Do not be anxious about anything, but in everything by prayer and supplication with thanksgiving let your requests be made known to God. And the peace of God, which surpasses all understanding, will guard your hearts and your minds in Christ Jesus" (Philippians 4:6-7).

Praying together can be a very intimate experience, both with your spouse and with God. But some couples don't know where to begin. That's why we're offering you this simple five-step process you can use to get started.

1. *Open with thanks.*
   - Thank God for showing up in the past and helping both you and your spouse.
   - Thank Him for creating the two of you and giving you the personalities and gifts you have.
   - Thank God for His promise to give you His peace when you bring your concerns to Him.

2. *Confess and submit.*
   - Confess your dependence on God for your life and the good things in it.
   - Express your desire to submit your will to His leadership and direction.
   - Ask Him to use your current situations to shape and mold you into the person He desires you to be.

3. *Seek God's direction.*
   - Ask God to guide you, your partner, and your family.
   - Ask Him to show both of you how to love and serve each other.
   - Ask God for guidance and direction so that His will may prevail as you both make important decisions.

4. *Pray for a bigger vision for your marriage.*
   - God desires your happiness together, but that's only part of His vision for married life. Ask Him to show the two of you how you can work together to serve Him.
   - Pray this prayer: "Lord, help me to see what You see, and help me to see what You want me to see."

5. *Close with thanks.*
   • Thank God for hearing your prayer and answering it according to His will.
   • Thank Him for your marriage and your opportunity to grow closer to each other and to Him.

Prayer isn't just something to do at church or in emergency "foxhole" situations. Prayer is part of life, and couples that make prayer part of their life together can experience a deeper love and sense of spiritual purpose together.

From Happiness to Oneness

Happy endings are expected in many stories and movies, but marriages based only on the pursuit of happiness often experience unhappiness.

God created both of you and brought you together for the journey of married life. The marriage you have experienced so far, be it good or bad, is not the end of the story. You are actually in the middle of writing a love story with your spouse and with God, and you get to write your part.

Instead of blaming your partner for failing to make you happy, focus some conversation on how the two of you can better help each other in your personal journeys through life, which is the supportive role of marriage.

Then spend some time discussing what you each think might be some of the things God is already doing, or wanting to do, through you as a couple. What are the opportunities through your lives and marriage where God can reveal Himself (the creative role of marriage)?

Remember, the Good News of Jesus Christ (the gospel) is never about how good we are, but rather what He is willing to do in us and through us, in spite of us and our many imperfections! Make sure you leave plenty of room for each of you, and for your marriage, to be an imperfect work in progress. As you do so, you may find yourself experiencing something that's even better than happiness: a deep and lasting joy, and a marriage filled with meaning and purpose.

LOVE LIE #2:

1 + 1 = 1

"We've got one hour, people. One hour!"

With the ceremony set to begin soon, both the wedding preparations and the wedding planner herself were in full swing.

"Move the table with the unity candle back a little and to the right," she instructed her assistant.

"That's it," she said. "Very nice. Now we just need the bride and groom to remember what they're supposed to do when the time comes."

Soon the ceremony was under way. The bride and groom perfectly executed their roles in the unity candle ceremony. They approached the table, where a thin white candle stood on either side of the larger unity candle. Each picked up one of the smaller candles and lit them. Then they simultaneously held their individual candles to light the unity candle.

This part of the wedding ceremony presents a beautiful image of two people becoming one. So far, so good.

In this particular case, the ritual ended with Ryan and Ashley blowing out their individual candles. The smoke from the two extinguished flames rose into the air, encircling the single flame of the unity candle. Now this couple would blend their two lives into one. Longed-for dreams were coming true.

Or were they?

Candles and Confusion

We've seen couples acting out the unity candle ritual in many of the weddings we've attended over the years. Sometimes the symbolism of the man and woman blowing out their individual candles is used for illustrative comments from the pulpit, such as, "Today, these two people are no longer two individual lives, but one flesh united in holy matrimony before God and these witnesses."

It's a beautiful ritual, but it drives us completely nuts! When we see the individual candles being blown out, we want to scream (but that would probably upset the bride, the groom, and the wedding guests). We want to pull out our hair (but that would bother the church janitors).

The main thing we want to do is rush to the altar and offer the bride and groom special discounts on our Marriage Intensives. They're probably going to need our help down the road because the beautiful unity candle ritual conceals a dangerous theological misunderstanding that can actually hinder these two lovers from achieving the unity and oneness they desire.

The problem happens at the very end of the ritual when the bride and groom blow out their individual candles. This symbolism strongly suggests that once these two individuals become one in marriage, they must suddenly cease being the two individuals they were before. It sends this message: *I no longer exist as an individual, but now my individuality and personality should be surrendered as we pursue the higher calling of becoming "one."*

Nobody's sure exactly where the whole unity candle trend

started. Most trace its rise to the 1981 wedding of Luke and Laura on the popular daytime TV soap opera *General Hospital*. Others say the whole trend took off because of creative candle merchants.

We would be absolutely fine if couples who light unity candles in their weddings could make one small but significant change to the ritual. Please, people, keep your two individual candles burning bright! This would send a much better message: *We are joining together in marriage to experience the unity and oneness marriage can bring, but the two of us are not obliterating our God-given individual existence or calling.*

It's a truly glorious event when two people become one flesh by coming together to create a new and mystical reality: the one flesh of marriage. But this event is not the end of two individuals. Each person still exists. And as we will see throughout this book, each one of them will have many important individual responsibilities to take care of in the coming years.

Jesus' teaching on marriage describes oneness as unity: "So they are no longer two but one flesh. What therefore God has joined together, let not man separate" (Matthew 19:6; see also Mark 10:1-8; 1 Corinthians 6:16; Ephesians 5:22-33). This Matthew verse uses the metaphor of "one flesh" to describe the spiritual, emotional, and physical unity we can experience only in marriage. But this metaphorical language should not be taken literally. That would be ridiculous.

Both of us have been married to our wives for decades, but so far, we and our spouses haven't morphed into conjoined twins. Each of us still have our own flesh, our own skin, our own brains, and our own hearts. We are *one* in marriage, but we are still *two* individuals.

This may seem like a small thing, or a distinction without a difference. But take it from us. The way we picture and imagine marriage is a *very big thing*.

Battle of the Marriage Models

In the popular online video game *Fortnite*, players seek a competitive advantage by firing up the hot-air balloon attached to their Battle Bus. As the Battle Bus rises high up into the sky, players can see the entire Battle Royale battlefield laid out before them and can plan their next moves accordingly. This superior perspective assists as they strategize and plan. Obviously, the better the game plan, the better the results.

It's the same in marriage. Most couples we talk to begin their marriages without any clear perspective of what they're really trying to accomplish together, or how to get there. However, we know that having a good perspective on the relational playing field and a sound marital strategy will always yield the best results.

In the game of marriage, we also have an Enemy who has his own perspective and game plan. If Satan can get men and women confused about God's design for marriage, they're more likely to build their union on faulty foundations. That's exactly what we see happening with many of the couples we serve.

In our work with troubled couples, we often find a flawed view of marriage, exemplified by the unity candle, underneath all the confusion and division. The unity candle ritual falsely says that "1 + 1 = 1." The fact is, there are three essential components in every marriage:

1. Man
2. Woman
3. Relationship

Successful marriages are those marriages where each of these three components is nurtured and cared for. Instead of doing away with our individual personalities as the unity candle suggests, a godly marriage flourishes when both the man and woman are healthy, flourishing, and burning bright!

Far from doing away with the individual man and woman, Jesus taught about the eternal significance of the man and the woman. They are eternal, but the relationship is not, because men and women will not be married in heaven (see Matthew 22:30 and Mark 12:25).

God's model for good marriages is built on three foundations: the man, the woman, and the relationship itself. All three must be nurtured and protected.

We need to change our equation.

It's not 1 + 1 = 1.

It's not 1 + 1 = 2.

It's 1 + 1 = 3. There's you and me and this thing called us.

This three-part model is one of the most shocking ideas we explore at our Marriage Intensives. We believe that it's God's math for marriage. As we work with this model, people actually get upset.

"Why have we never seen this before!"

"If we had only understood this before we got married, our whole relationship would have been so much easier and healthier."

Most people don't actually draw diagrams of how their relationship is structured, so let us lead you through a few illustrations to help you get your perspective. Fire up the hot-air balloon. We're going to fly high in the sky for a moment so we can better visualize God's plan for marriage.

The image of two becoming one needs to be traded for a model with three parts. That's our plan here. Building toward that end, though, we will first contrast our upcoming picture of a healthy marriage with the two more common distortions. Let's display those models graphically, using a theoretical couple we'll call Ryan and Ashley.

Marriage Model #1: Two Become One

First, let's take a look at the popular two-become-one model.

THEY MEET

Ryan   Ashley

Here we see Ryan (that attractive figure on the left) meeting Ashley (an equally stunning figure).

Apparently, Ryan and Ashley like each other very much. They fall in love and decide to get married. They blow out their individual candles during the unity candle ritual, and so they envision their marriage like this.

TWO BECOME ONE

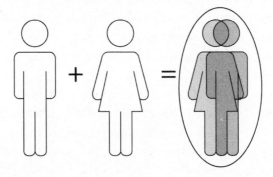

First, we had individual figures for Ryan and Ashley, but now it appears to be only one figure inside the dotted lines of the relationship circle. This is the way Ryan and Ashley picture the two of them becoming one.

This two-become-one model may sound good in theory, but it stinks in real marriages. Not only is "1 + 1 = 1" bad math, but it's not possible! The problem: When Ryan and Ashley look at this model, each asks, "Hey, where did I go?" Or, "Where did you go?" Somebody gets eliminated.

Sadly, I (Bob) bought a version of this idea hook, line, and sinker! For me it subtly took the form of a belief that marriages were far better when the couple had more in common than less. Differences, therefore, were typically seen as a significant source of trouble and needed to be resolved and overcome. Sounds reasonable, doesn't it?

This belief was clearly evident one day about nine years into our marriage. In those days the differences between me and my wife, Jenni, collided frequently, and we fought a lot! Normally, when I would get upset about something, I would try to help Jenni see why her position and feelings were wrong and how she needed to change.

We had recently taken a neighbor family into our home for a couple of months when they unexpectedly had fallen on hard times. This forced us to attempt to remain on our best behavior and not demonstrate in full color the uglier sides of ourselves and our marriage.

Our normal pattern was predictable. When differences arose, I would try to persuade Jenni to accept my idea of resolution. (At that point in our marriage, I was relatively oblivious to my deeper objective of getting her to think and feel more like I did.) Jenni, then, would commonly escalate into anger in an attempt to get me to back off. But now, because of our guests, she wasn't willing to use that method.

For a while she simply tried to avoid me in order to keep us from fighting. Unfortunately, that didn't seem to be working well enough, so she had to get creative. Hoping a new angle might actually get through to me, she bought greeting cards that expressed the emotions she was having. She thought that these cards just might help my emotionally dense head hear what was happening in her heart.

One day while looking through her cards, she came to the realization that we just saw things *differently*. On the day in question, we got sideways over something, and she asked me if I was willing to walk to the park so she could share her new understanding.

I agreed. When we got to the park, she took out a piece of paper and drew a line down the middle. She labeled one side "Bob" and the other side "Jenni." On the "Bob" side, she listed the way I saw the issue we were arguing about. On the other side, she listed the way she saw it.

She then asked me if I agreed with the way she had described it. I acknowledged that what she listed on both sides was accurate. Then Jenni said, "From my perspective you just see this differently than I do. And I'm okay with the way you see it. Can you be okay with the way I see it?" My answer was an emphatic "No!"

Jenni was absolutely shocked by my response. In her mind, differences were an acceptable and natural part of all human relationships. However, at that point I was thoroughly locked into a belief that they were a problem to overcome! Unconsciously I was operating under the relational math equation that $1 + 1 = 1$, making *differences* the enemy!

We have worked with many couples who embrace the $1 + 1 = 1$ lie. Our experience shows this model just doesn't work. It doesn't provide men and women with a meaningful model for caring for each other or for their marriage relationship. And also, typically, when God combines things together, their sum is greater than their parts, not less.

Let's compare this with a slightly improved model that many people adopt.

Marriage Model #2: Two Marry and Remain Two

One alternative to the 1 + 1 = 1 lie is the "two remain two" model. This model recognizes that there are still two people in the marriage after the couple says, "I do." That model looks like this.

THEY MEET

Dave   Kelly

They are one in marriage, but they remain two individuals.

At first glance, Dave and Kelly seem like a normal couple. They meet, fall in love, get married, and now they're raising three teenagers and one goldendoodle named Sammy. They exercise in the morning, see the kids off to school, go to work, eat meals, watch their favorite TV shows, attend church, enjoy the outdoors, participate in hobbies, and socialize with friends.

Except there's a problem: They do all of these things on their own.

Married for seventeen years, Dave and Kelly have grown independent from each other and have been leading separate lives for years. Dave is immersed in his career as a commercial pilot, taking the kids to practices, and playing golf; Kelly is absorbed in working as a teacher, raising their three children, managing household responsibilities, and socializing with friends.

Their marriage feels cold and distant—like they're speeding down two parallel tracks instead of living one life together. Both are fiercely independent, and their priority isn't the marriage relationship. After a whirlwind romance and wedding, they quickly had their first child. They never really had an opportunity to learn how to be a connected couple. Now, the majority of their time and energy goes into their jobs and their children. Their primary mission together is to raise happy, well-adjusted kids who follow the Lord. They are great parents but lousy lovers, content to share a home and bills but not an interconnected relationship. The only time they are together is at a child's sporting event, church, or when they need to discuss finances, logistics, schedules, or to-do lists.

Dave and Kelly occasionally fantasize about finding someone else, but they stay married because loneliness isn't biblical grounds for divorce (see Matthew 19:9), and they don't want to hurt their children. They both came from broken homes and can't stand the thought of their kids experiencing the pain of divorce.

TWO MARRY AND REMAIN TWO

This model is marginally better than 1 + 1 = 1. At least neither of the participants has been eliminated. But this view is still riddled with pitfalls. It unknowingly sets people up for a life of frustration, loneliness, and pain. We like the fact that there are two people inside the marriage relationship circle. Sadly, though, this model is built upon many of the lies we'll soon be sharing.

Marriage Model #3: Two Marry, and Much More Is Going On!

When we work with married couples, we try to help them understand and embrace a different model of marriage. Our Healthy Marriage Model has a few more components to it but provides a clearer picture of God's eternal design for marriage. We actually find it to be truer to real married life and far easier to make work.

If Ryan and Ashley began their married life with our improved model in mind, they would have a more complete view of what marriage is and possess better strategies for dealing with the challenges they'll likely face. We believe it sets them up with a winning game plan.

So that you have a clear understanding of this new model, let's build it piece by piece. We'll start with the basics and then apply it to Ryan and Ashley.

The Healthy Adult

First, you'll need to know about the foundational building block of a healthy marriage: the healthy adult.

We'll be talking more about various aspects of healthy adulthood throughout the book, but for now let's keep it simple. If any of us hope to have a healthy marriage, the best starting place is two healthy individuals. We would be the first to confess this model is something of an ideal, so don't get discouraged if you see yourself at a different starting place. The same is generally true of most of us, but stick with us here.

What do we mean by healthy? The shortest answer is that these are two fully functioning adults. The key feature is full responsibility. Seems simple enough, doesn't it? Believe it or not, though, most people we talk with have never really thoroughly thought through what it means to be an adult, let alone would be able to clearly articulate a definition.

This adult component is so central to our understanding of God's design for marriage, it seems worth the time to first offer our definition. Then we'll take a minute to show how we got there.

We define an adult as a person *capable* of fully caring for their whole being (physical, mental, emotional, and spiritual), who has also accepted full *responsibility* for the job. So a true adult is *capable* and *responsible* for themselves first, as you can see in the illustration that follows.

HEALTHY ADULT

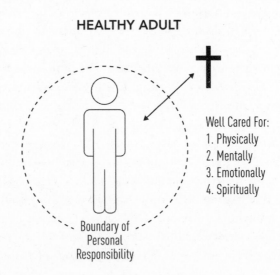

Well Cared For:
1. Physically
2. Mentally
3. Emotionally
4. Spiritually

Boundary of
Personal
Responsibility

So how did we arrive at this definition? Here's our thinking. We all enter the world as helpless children, completely dependent on others (when possible, loving parents) to provide all we need to survive and thrive. In a perfect world, at first our parents attend to all of our physical, mental, emotional, and spiritual needs so that we remain healthy and well cared for.

As we grow, however, we become increasingly able to do things for ourselves. Good, effective parents support our growth and development by doing less for us as we become able, and they encourage us to learn to care for ourselves. This is the primary responsibility of parenting.

In addition to helping us learn and grow, there is a second key component of quality parenting. Really good parents also provide ongoing modeling of what responsible self-care, in all four key areas of life, actually looks like. For all humans, learning to do anything well is made far easier when we see it done. Nothing helps a child learn to be a responsible adult better than watching their parents do it well.

Thus, people most effectively prepare for adulthood through a solid combination of watching and doing. With excellent modeling, lots of trial and error, and a good dose of practice, we learn to become fully functioning adults. The day of graduation to adulthood, therefore, occurs when we're fully capable of caring for ourselves and finally declare, "From this day forward the entire job of caring for me is now mine: physically, mentally, emotionally, and spiritually, and I'm on it!" And while nothing helps a child become an adult better than good modeling, we're also saying that nothing helps a marriage become great more than being a union between healthy adults.

Sounds simple, right? We wish it were, but sadly it's not. Most of us have been cheated. As we look around us and work with struggling couples, we've noticed that both this understanding of true adulthood, and the modeling of it, is largely missing.

We both get to frequently speak to large groups of people. We commonly ask this question: "Would anybody in the crowd who had even one parent consistently demonstrate what it looked like to expertly and responsibly care for themselves in all four areas please raise your hand." Startlingly, no one normally raises their hand. Only occasionally are even one or two hands lifted among the hundreds who don't. Let that soak in!

So if we've never seen it modeled, how are we supposed to even know it's our job, let alone know what it looks like? Our understanding of adulthood, as a result, gets distorted or is completely absent.

Add to that the fact we live in a society that not only teaches but romanticizes a fairy-tale view of marriage. The story suggests that if we can just find the right person to meet all our needs, we can live happily ever after. Since we are generally not taught what it means to be a responsible adult first—and with the fairy tale beckoning—it only makes sense that we would look to both our spouse and our marriage to be a key source of our happiness and fulfillment. As we will soon show, this is a big setup!

So where's the hope? Well, the good news about adulthood is that it is fundamentally about just two things: *capability* and *responsibility*. If you are *able* to care well for yourself, and then take on the job, you qualify. Those of us with less-than-ideal modeling may have to work a little harder to figure it out, but it's completely doable. So, in essence, to be a healthy adult you don't have to fully have it together yet; you just have to be willing and able.

And we can make it even easier. There happens to be one more important element to being a fully functioning, healthy adult: recognizing that, by design, we are dependent upon God. In fact, our very life and breath is only maintained as God's hand of sustaining grace remains upon us. This is really great news because He can provide so much of what we need, including what we didn't get growing up (more on this to come). Thus, the job of an effective adult is to balance responsibly caring for ourselves while simultaneously depending on the Lord, who is our ultimate source of life, strength, wisdom, and knowledge.

In the healthy adult diagram, the circle around the adult stick figure represents a 24-7 personal responsibility for health and well-being. Within his or her own circle, the person consistently cares for self in all areas. The arrow indicates he or she also continually maintains and utilizes the essential life-giving relationship with God.

Now, back to Ryan and Ashley. They don't need to be Olympic athletes, Mensa scholars, fully actualized individuals, or saints to qualify as adults. In fact, we're all imperfect people with our own issues to overcome. If either of them is overweight, prone to fits of rage, or convinced there's no such thing as God, such issues in one or more of the four areas will certainly affect them as individuals. It would also naturally tax the health of any relationship they found themselves in.

As we have seen, for either of them to have any real hope of having a truly healthy marriage, Ryan and Ashley must at least be on the road to becoming healthier people. That's what an adult does. Like us, they don't need to be perfect and sinless to enter marriage. They're normal, imperfect people from normal, imperfect families with normal, imperfect parents.

However, like many of the people we work with, something woke each of them up and they took on the job of independently becoming functional adults. Through their commitment to personal responsibility and self-care, they now become people capable of forging a strong marriage.

When Two Healthy Adults Meet
If Ryan and Ashley started off with a sound marriage model instead of the flawed 1 + 1 = 1 model they embraced during their wedding's unity candle ritual, they would see their relationship like this.

TWO HEALTHY ADULTS MEET

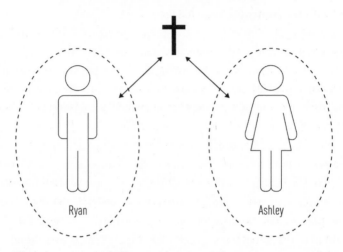

There's a major difference between this marriage model and models one and two. Here, each individual is within his or her own relationship circle. That's because Ryan has a healthy relationship with himself, where he listens to and cares for himself throughout the day, and Ashley has a similar healthy relationship with herself. Instead of disappearing into each other, each remains a responsible individual—a healthy adult.

We realize that for some readers the idea of having a relationship with yourself may be a new idea, so let's pause and share our basic perspective on this important concept. In general, a good relationship between two people has to do with how they interact with each other and what results. For example, does the way they interact encourage and support health and well-being; lead to a deeper, useful, and more satisfying connection; and contribute to healing, growth, and purpose? All of the above and more are components of a quality relationship and can help us assess where we are and consider what we can do to make it better. Obviously, this only occurs when the couple makes a realistic appraisal of the good, the bad, and the ugly, and then does more of the good and attends to the bad and the ugly. Likewise, as we grow up and become adults, every one of us has a relationship with our self. It could be a healthy relationship or an unhealthy one.

For example, if Ryan goes through every day listening to his own mind and heart, seeking to understand what's going on inside, he is on his way to developing a healthy relationship with himself. On the other hand, if Ryan is doubtful and self-critical and spends each day engaging in negative self-talk, his relationship with himself is less healthy.

The same goes for Ryan's spiritual health. If he is really treating himself well, he will live with a continual awareness that he is more than physical—he is a spiritual being involved in an essential, life-giving relationship with God. As Christians, we also know that this must include our recognition of the many ways we are still flawed and imperfect and thus need God's grace as we hopefully let Him help us become a little more like Him every day. If Ryan ignores his spiritual health, it's like he's trying to run his life on his own power instead of staying plugged in to God's inexhaustible power supply.

The same goes for Ashley, over there in her own relationship circle. If she goes through every day listening to her own mind and heart, seeking to better understand what's going on inside herself, she will remain whole, healthy, and cared for, overflowing with an abundance of good and loving engagement with everyone she meets each day. She knows that treating herself with care and respect means remaining connected to her true source. This is what the picture of two healthy adults seeks to convey.

Two Healthy Adults Build a Healthy Relationship

Let's review what has happened with Ryan and Ashley so far. Both of them have healthy relationships with themselves. Both of them have healthy relationships with Christ. Now they want to create a healthy relationship with each other.

As Ashley and Ryan decide to build a friendship, another layer of detail is added to our marriage model. In addition to their personal circles, there's now a new relationship circle: the Interactive Space. This is where their friendship will grow. They enter into a relationship with each other and embark on the beginnings of an intimate journey.

TWO HEALTHY ADULTS BUILD A HEALTHY RELATIONSHIP

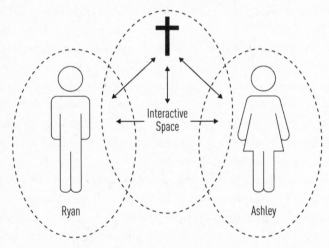

Intimacy is a commonly misunderstood concept, so to avoid confusion let's define what we mean. Frequently today it's used as a reference to sex, but we're referring to a far richer and deeper meaning. Our definition is also much broader. This may even take some of you a few moments to get used to. We use the term *intimacy* to connect to the biblical understanding of *knowing*, as in the idea of knowing and being known. This more subtle definition has profound implications when couples strive to build a solid friendship. And we're convinced that truly great marriages have a good friendship at their base.

When Ryan and Ashley first met, they began to get to know each other. They entered into the Interactive Space and their initial and shallow "intimate" encounter was merely an exchange of names. But notice, an engagement between two previous strangers took place. This is the beginning of their relationship.

Within this Interactive Space the relationship develops as Ashley and Ryan learn more about each other by sharing who they are, what they like, and what they want to do in life. If things seem good and they want to go deeper still, they might discuss their dreams and aspirations, their passions, and their sense of life calling.

Thus, intimacy becomes the journey of getting to know each other in deeper and deeper ways over time. Intimacy can certainly incorporate sexuality at some point in the journey, but it is much more than a physical relationship. It is a relationship between the hearts, minds, bodies, and spirits of two people. As a result, we'll show in a moment why God designed sex, and some of the other deep elements of intimacy, to warrant an additional relational layer of protection and commitment.

Ryan and Ashley are on a journey of intimacy. They are getting to know each other and allowing themselves to be known in deeper and deeper ways over time. As their friendship grows, they are experiencing a deepening bond and connection, along with a growing feeling of closeness and security.

Any time they are apart, they temporarily leave this Interactive Space. In fact, both Ryan and Ashley move in and out of this space throughout the day. If Ryan calls Ashley from work and they have any exchange, they are entering this space even though they are not face-to-face.

All normal, healthy relationships include a continual moving in and out of this space. Since this is the space they occupy together, where they actually engage, for the relationship to continue to grow this space needs constant attention to make it one they both enjoy being in.

If the Interactive Space feels tense, or filled with anger, or they anticipate criticism, hurtful interactions, or other unpleasant experiences, they'll likely be apprehensive to enter. If, however, the space is warm, cozy, exciting, loving, and pleasurable, they'll be far more likely to want to go in. They each get to do their part to help create an interactive environment they both feel comfortable in and look forward to spending time in.

Over time, this is where many couples encounter trouble. Having initially created a warm and vibrant Interactive Space, they neglect it, assuming it will continue to grow on its own. But their relationship can't grow on its own any more than a garden can. For their relationship to continue growing, they must regularly enter the Interactive Space together and invest time and energy into keeping the relationship alive. This is where they can cultivate a friendship they love. If not, the relationship may wither and die for lack of attention. This is how couples typically drift apart.

But let's say that Ryan and Ashley continue to grow closer together in the four main areas: mental, emotional, physical, and spiritual. They enjoy regular life-giving communication, affection, fun times, laughter, outside friendships, making decisions as a team, and successfully working through the inevitable conflicts and crises.

When two healthy adults are building a relationship with each other and with God, they can also experience a vibrant, shared spiritual experience together. Couples can invest in their spiritual intimacy by turning their private times with God into times where they interact with God *together*. This can include prayer, devotions,

Bible study, church and Sunday school attendance, discussions about God and their faith journeys, and many other rich opportunities that can deepen their intimate relationship with God.

When two people experience intimacy by knowing and being known by each other, they also have an opportunity to experience and know Him *together*, to grow spiritually *together*.

Two Healthy Adults Create a Healthy Marriage

Ryan and Ashley's marriage ceremony was so beautiful that no one noticed the missing unity candle ritual. Getting married hasn't caused their individual personalities to disappear. They no longer buy that lie. Both of them still exist.

As we congratulate the happy couple, let's take a look at our final addition to our marriage model. See that new solid circle around Ryan and Ashley's relationship? We call that the Covenant Marriage Boundary.

TWO HEALTHY ADULTS CREATE A HEALTHY MARRIAGE

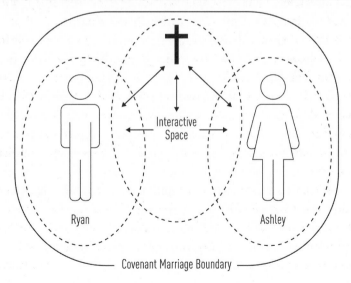

Today, many men and women of marrying age are skipping marriage and are living together. "Why get married?" many of them ask.

Men and women can experience levels of intimacy without marriage, but when Ryan and Ashley looked at each other and said, "I do," they were making a complete commitment. They were "all in." They were devoting themselves to each other until death do them part.

This level of commitment requires its own circle in our marriage model. People have many relationships in life. Some are deep, while some are more superficial. With their marriage, Ryan and Ashley are making a commitment to go deep, to let their partner enter in to their heart of hearts, to fully know and be known.

These parts of us that are so valuable are also vulnerable. As we reveal our heart to another person, we reveal our fears and weaknesses, our doubts and deficiencies, and our spiritual gifts and character traits. But we also reveal that our heart was made like God's—a heart that can be broken. We are vulnerable when we share these valuable aspects of ourselves with our partner because things of great value can be easily damaged and devalued. Each person risks being devalued, mistreated, and damaged.

With so much at stake, our marriage model needed another circle, another layer of protection and security. God designed marriage between a man and a woman to be a reflection of the marriage between Christ (the Bridegroom) and His people, the church (His bride). God calls us to seal this marriage union with a promise, a vow, a covenant. This promise is represented by the outer circle in the diagram, the Covenant Marriage Boundary.

This circle came into view during their wedding when Ryan and Ashley looked at each other and said, "Never will I leave you; never will I forsake you." This covenant is a promise and a pledge. "I will always care for you. I will never leave you. Our Interactive Space is a sacred place I will guard and protect against all enemies." This is true security.

The promise of marriage can create a level of safety and security that enables us to be open and vulnerable enough to know each other and be known deeply, just as the first couple experienced in the Garden. Adam and Eve were "both naked and were not ashamed" (Genesis 2:25). Ashley and Ryan are committed to making their Interactive Space one of the safest places on earth!

This safe and secure space is the place God designed for sexual intimacy. Sex is a physical expression of the deep and intimate connections Ryan and Ashley already experience in the other areas of their lives. When sexuality is expressed within the safety and security of the Covenant Marriage Boundary, this intimacy can grow to its deepest level.

A Marriage Model That Works

We have reviewed three of the major marriage models people carry around in their heads. Let's do a quick review.

1 + 1 = 1 Model

It sounds wonderful, and it addresses God's plan for men and women to experience oneness, but this model fails to account for other important elements. Most problematic is the "Where Did I Go?" issue that happens when two people join in marriage, but only one person is represented.

1 + 1 = 2 Model

This model is a slight improvement. At least neither Ryan nor Ashley disappears. But this model creates separate lives where the two individuals end up feeling lonely—like married roommates.

1 + 1 = 3 Model

Finally, here's a model that's robust and realistic. The essential elements are all here, including:

- two healthy adults,
- each of whom has a relationship with himself or herself,
- and each of whom has a close relationship with Christ, who is their sustainer.
- The two adults meet and develop a relationship, indicated by the shared Interactive Space between them that consists of meaningful communication, time together, fun and laughter, managing conflict in a healthy way, sexual intimacy, and a shared spiritual relationship (safety);
- they marry, creating a Covenant Marriage Boundary around their relationship (security);
- and Christ is present and active in this healthy relationship.

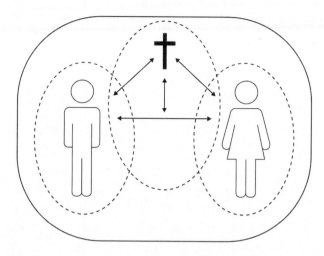

Both partners are committed to being healthy adults in the four areas: physical, mental, spiritual, and emotional. And both are committed to doing their part to actively deepen and strengthen their shared Interactive Space so that both enjoy and feel safe within this center circle.

These two flawed and imperfect people are on a journey of marital love. They're more fully becoming who they were created to be, different by design; they are knowing and being known; they love, care for, and support each other. This is intimacy at its best! The two have become one in spirit and purpose, but there's so much more going on.

Jenni and I (Bob) have come a long way from the days of greeting cards and my animosity toward our differences. God has repeatedly demonstrated to me how magnificent His design for marriage actually is. I have become so grateful for the reality that Jenni and I are *really* different! Our diversity of design not only brings color and adventure to our lives; it frequently brings benefits we would have otherwise missed alone.

One fun example of our marriage successfully enjoying the 1 + 1 = 3 equation occurred a few years ago, when the Lord helped us overcome a common source of tension: planning our vacations. You see, Jenni and I have very different ideas about what an ideal vacation is. Jenni loves to go, and do, and see as much as possible. Now I love to travel and see new things, but when we did vacations Jenni's way, I came home exhausted, needing a vacation from our vacation!

By contrast, my ideal vacation is to find a beautiful, scenic beach where I can relax, sun, and swim, with no agenda or time-lines. I work hard, under constant appointments and deadlines, and really need time to relax and recharge. Doing little or nothing meaningful is the key for me.

It doesn't take much creativity to see the fertile ground for constant conflict in our marriage around our vacations. But God had a better plan we finally uncovered, and our differences turned out to be gold.

That particular year Jenni and I decided to use the methods Greg and I developed (which will be revealed and expanded throughout this book) to hear each other's hearts and better manage conflict. After talking about how we each felt about vacations, what each other's preferences were, and why we felt that way, we decided to try to create a vacation that we could both love.

As a result, we strategically planned out our road trip to Yellowstone and Grand Teton National Parks in a way we had never done before: day on, day off, day on, day off. The "on" days were packed full of sightseeing and experiences that would leave us fulfilled and exhausted. The "off" days were all about relaxing, recharging, perhaps sitting around a body of water, and just existing at a slower pace.

In the end, we both agreed it was the best vacation ever! We also learned that Jenni's natural tendency to be on the go can frequently cause her to overplan and overdo it, even with her amazing stamina. And I am capable of underdoing to the point of boredom, just because I'm so determined to chill out. What we discovered, instead, was that when we allow our differences to blend, we now commonly find ways of operating as a couple that are far better than either would have found alone. We both now know we are really better together.

This vacation example is one simple expression of the many benefits we now experience daily as a result of our friendship, as we appreciate and take advantage of the diversity God created between us. Thus, for us now in so many ways, our marriage math is not 1 + 1 = 1 or 1 + 1 = 2, but something more than the sum of us: 1 + 1 = 3.

Get used to this model, because we are going to refer back to it throughout this book. The details may escape you, but remember these three essential components in every marriage:

1. Man
2. Woman
3. Relationship

When all three are healthy, you and your spouse will experience the joy and beauty of marriage as God designed it.

LOVE LIE #3:

ALL YOU NEED IS LOVE

We're leading a Marriage Intensive, and right now, it's Brittany and Jon's turn to talk.

The two of them *totally agree* on one thing: Something vital is missing from their relationship. They still care for each other, but the passionate feelings they once had for each other seem to have cooled or gone on long-term vacation. Their theme song could be the Righteous Brothers' 1964 hit, "You've Lost That Lovin' Feelin'."

But Brittany and Jon *totally disagree* about everything else. They have different diagnoses of what has happened to them. They have differing prescriptions for how they can turn things around. Here's a condensed version of the analysis and action plans they presented during the session.

Brittany's Viewpoint

Brittany feels the problem is crystal clear: heart chemistry. "The chemistry between us is just gone," she says. "When we dated and early in our marriage, we enjoyed a passionate love that would literally take my breath away. But not anymore."

She has promoted ideas about how to regain the spark they once had. Her fear, though, is that if that chemistry is gone, can it ever return? For years she's tried to reinject passion into their marriage by having more date nights, getting away for weekend romantic getaways, and being more relaxed and adventurous in their lovemaking. But now she reports, "I just don't know if I even love Jon anymore."

Brittany sees love as an intense, almost magical emotional experience that unites two people in marriage. It's either there, or it's not. She has long wished Jon would join her in reigniting the flaming embers of their love. Now she's afraid it might be too late.

Jon's Viewpoint

Jon sees another culprit: lack of decisive commitment. Jon's a big fan of Greg's dad, Christian marriage counselor Gary Smalley. Jon has been studying and trying to apply the lessons of Gary's bestselling book *Love Is a Decision*. Jon underlined and highlighted one paragraph from the book's opening chapter:

> Whether it's a family, a school, a company, or a sports team, we cannot possibly guide our relationships safely through the waters of our day without a plan. That's the starting point. Without a clear plan of action that points out the way to the deep waters of intimacy and avoids the shallow rocks of marital ruin we're inviting heartache into our homes. It's critical that we clearly plan our lives and not let chance set the course.[1]

As Jon sees it, love is something that develops between two people who decide to love each other. Yes, it's a feeling, but a feeling that flows from their decision. It's not something that just spontaneously erupts between two people. "Feelings can change as quickly as the wind blows," says Jon. "That's no foundation to build a marriage on."

Jon believes that for a marriage in the twenty-first century to survive, there needs to be something holding it together that's stronger and more stable than two people's ever-fluctuating emotional states. That foundation is laid when two people decide to love each other.

Different Approaches

Jon and Brittany agree that love is essential, but they disagree about what love is and how they can keep it alive in their marriage. It's not uncommon for husbands and wives to view and approach love and marriage in different ways, but it can make for very difficult rowing. When two people in a rowboat row in the same direction, there's a good chance they can arrive at their destination. But when they row in opposite directions, there's plenty of commotion but no forward progress. In fact, they end up going in circles.

If Brittany and Jon don't figure out how to start rowing together in the same direction, they risk suffering a cascading series of unpleasant consequences:

- Feeling trapped and frustrated in a marriage that doesn't seem to be growing or going anywhere
- Deciding that since they can't work things out together, both partners will try their best to work things out on their own
- Experiencing a gap between them that grows wider over time

- Living in a marriage made of two increasingly lonely people instead of a marriage where two people love each other *and* their marriage
- Looking for love in all the wrong places

After we wrap up Jon and Brittany's talk time, our intensive group breaks for lunch. But before we (Bob and Greg) eat, we quickly compare mental notes on what we just heard and saw. We totally agree about three points.

First, we can understand why Brittany describes love as chemistry, because we largely experience emotions through complex chemical processes in our minds and bodies—processes that can literally take a person's breath away. But love is so much more than good chemistry.

Second, we can see why Jon describes love as a decision. The good and bad decisions partners make have real impact on their relationship. But love is so much more than decisions.

And third, Brittany and Jon are both missing the most important thing there is to know about love: It comes from God *and* it is God.

Understanding Love: Feeling or Decision?

It was June 1967—still early in the so-called "Summer of Love"— when the Beatles unveiled their new song "All You Need Is Love" to an audience of four hundred million people in twenty-five countries as part of the world's first live global television event.

The Beatles wanted to do more than sing a pretty song. They wanted to make a statement and possibly change the world. But these desires did little to heal the disputes raging within the world's most famous rock band. As Christian rocker Larry Norman would later observe: "Beatles said All you need is love, and then they broke up."[2]

What is love? The answers you find will depend on where you look. When you answer the question with pop songs and love poetry, feelings and "chemistry" reign supreme.

"My love is such that rivers cannot quench," wrote Anne Bradstreet in her classic poem "To My Dear and Loving Husband."

Love poems also explore the feelings that remain after love is gone, as Robert Louis Stevenson showed in "Love, What Is Love?"

Love—what is love? A great and aching heart;
Wrung hands; and silence; and a long despair.

Others insist love is more decision than chemistry. Erich Fromm promoted this idea in his 1956 book, *The Art of Loving*: "[Love] is a decision, it is a judgment, it is a promise. If love were only a feeling, there would be no basis for the promise to love each other forever. A feeling comes and it may go. How can I judge that it will stay forever, when my act does not involve judgment and decision?"[3] And even though Fromm declared love was a decision, he did not create a plan of action for achieving it, as he admitted near the end of *The Art of Loving*: "I am afraid that any-one who approaches this last chapter in this spirit will be gravely disappointed."[4]

But Gary Smalley and other Christian writers were happy to give Christian readers blueprints they could follow. Gary explained his goal early in *Love Is a Decision:* "That's what this book is all about. It's our best effort to give you a workable, biblically based plan of action for building loving, lasting relationships."[5]

Gary never would have suggested marrying someone you didn't like and then deciding to love that partner by sheer force of will, but that's the way some people make him sound. Here's how one blogger adopted the love-is-a-decision model: "Love is a decision you make and continue to make in order to create an experience that is described as love. . . . Love is something [you] do, not something you feel."[6]

It's hard for love to grow in marriage when partners embrace fundamentally different concepts of what it is and how it works. However, nothing makes it harder for love to grow than missing the basic understanding of what love really is and how it works.

Our Answer to the Riddle of the Ages!

When people ask us whether love is a feeling or a decision, we frustrate some of them when we give them our answer: Yes!

Yes, love is a decision. We are not claiming that you can decide your way to love, but we do believe certain decisions can help love flourish. As shown in the last chapter, the vows couples recite in their wedding ceremonies illustrate the decisions they've made to protect their relationship:

"You are the one for me, and I want to spend the rest of my life with you."

"I am going to love you and be by your side, no matter what happens."

"I will remain faithful to you by cutting off all other romantic options."

"I am yours."

Decisions like these can create safe and nurturing environments where the deepest love can grow. But decisions alone don't create love. Think about it: If love is only a decision, it's destined to remain up in your brain.

Yes, love is a feeling, perhaps one of the most powerful and enjoyable feelings we can experience. Love is such a powerful feeling that it impacts all the other feelings we have. When you feel you are loved, your whole world looks better. You feel elevated. It feels good to be alive. Anything seems possible.

Feelings are essential to love, but feelings alone are not strong enough to sustain and support a healthy and stable marriage through the many challenges of life. In fact, feelings good and bad will ebb and flow. If the health of the relationship were based on the strength and consistency of the feelings, every marriage would be unstable!

Brittany and Jon's differences over whether love is chemistry or decision-based may reflect their differences in personality types. Some people are dominant feelers while some are dominant thinkers. That's fine. God doesn't wire us all the same way, and He designed marriage to accommodate all our differences and perspectives.

Now that we have settled the decision/feeling issue that has divided spouses and philosophers for centuries, let's take a closer look at this crazy little thing called love.

God's Glorious Gift

Many people think love is something that happens between two people, but that's only part of the story. Love is actually a much bigger story. It's an older story, too. Love has been around for a very long time. In fact, love existed before people did, before God created the cosmos.

Christians have a unique opportunity to experience love because they are connected to the main source: *God is the creator of love and God is love.*

John was the disciple of love. He wrote frequently about the subject and was also described as the disciple Jesus loved (see John 13:23). In his first epistle, John explains that love is the foundation of our relationship with God:

> Beloved, let us love one another, for love is from God, and whoever loves has been born of God and knows God. Anyone who does not love does not know God, because God is love. . . . Beloved, if God so loved us, we also ought to love one another. No one has ever seen

God; if we love one another, God abides in us and his
love is perfected in us.

1 JOHN 4:7-8, 11-12

The Bible often instructs or commands us to love like this. As God's *beloved* (which means "much loved"), we are told to love God, our neighbor, our enemies, our spouse, and our children. But we can't make ourselves love someone on command, can we?

We don't control love. We can't manufacture love. Nor can we make someone else love us, because they can't manufacture love either. We can certainly pressure and manipulate other people in an effort to make them do what we want, but that's hardly the best environment for true love to grow.

The most important thing we can do is receive God's love, drink it in thoroughly, and then allow it to pass through us to others. Stop thinking of love as something that originates in your heart and is then passed on to someone else. Instead, think of love as something that comes from God, flows throughout the cosmos 24-7, and even flows through you.

We don't need to work on forcing love when it's so abundant. We merely need to open our hearts to tap into the source, let it flow into our parched souls, and let it flow through us to bring love to everyone we meet.

Love is really neither a feeling nor a decision. It's a free-flowing gift that you can only receive and pass on. It starts when you open your heart to God and accept His love. It continues when you open your heart to the people around you and let that divine love flow through you to them. Thus, when you really love someone, it's not your love you feel and share—it's God's.

Part of Jon and Brittany's struggle is they know they need love, but they haven't really understood what it is and where it comes from. Chemistry and decisions may help, but the two of them can't simply conjure the chemistry or make the decision to love each other more. They've tried, but they realize they can't force it.

There is one thing they can do: open up and invite love (God) in. Then they can follow by opening their hearts to each other. People with open hearts allow love to flow in from God and flow right back out in loving actions toward other people. Marriages based on this foundation can grow and flourish, because this is how God designed it all to work.

Next let's take a moment to look into our heart condition, and then we'll get practical. Our goal is to assist you to more fully and *safely* open your heart in order to receive all that the Lord has for you. It will allow you to be a better reflection of who He created you to be. We have found that great marriages are significantly advanced when each person is able to remain more open and "plugged in."

Self-Assessment: Is Your Heart Open to Love?

It's time for a heart checkup. Answer the following questions to see if your heart is open and ready for love to flow through. The goal here is to do a brief self-evaluation, not to criticize yourself or your spouse. Here is a chance to get to know yourself and your spouse better and to identify where new opportunities exist.

1. How open would you say your heart is to the following?

   a. My heart is open to God and His love:

1	2	3	4	5	6	7	8	9	10
Closed				Sometimes					Open

   b. My heart is open to my spouse:

1	2	3	4	5	6	7	8	9	10
Closed				Sometimes					Open

c. My heart is open to other people in my world:

1	2	3	4	5	6	7	8	9	10
Closed				Sometimes					Open

2. What about your family of origin? Did you see these kinds of love expressed in your family?

a. My family expressed love for God:

1	2	3	4	5	6	7	8	9	10
Never				Sometimes					Always

b. My parents expressed love between husband and wife:

1	2	3	4	5	6	7	8	9	10
Never				Sometimes					Always

c. My family experienced love between our parents and the children:

1	2	3	4	5	6	7	8	9	10
Never				Sometimes					Always

d. My parents and family members expressed love for others in the community:

1	2	3	4	5	6	7	8	9	10
Never				Sometimes					Always

3. What about your marriage? How would you say your marriage has impacted your heart? Choose the best answer below and explain your answer.

a. My marriage has helped me open my heart to greater love for God, my spouse, and others:

1	2	3	4	5	6	7	8	9	10
Never				Sometimes					Always

Explain.

b. Problems in my marriage have motivated me to close my heart to greater experiences of love:

1	2	3	4	5	6	7	8	9	10
Never				Sometimes					Always

Explain.

4. Heart-closers. Have you experienced any of the following problems? All of these challenges put people and their hearts under pressure. Which ones have you been facing?

- Financial problems
- Depression or anxiety
- Busyness and the hectic pace of life
- Feeling tired or not getting enough sleep and rest
- Chaos or stress

- Negative self-talk ("I'm such an idiot!" or "I will never be able to do that!")
- Hunger, illness, or low blood sugar
- Fear or loneliness
- Grief over the loss of a loved one

5. What about your marriage dynamics? Which of the following relational warning signs show up between you and your partner?

- Lack of eye contact
- Folded or crossed arms, or other negative body language
- Avoiding touch
- Withdrawing
- Attacking each other
- Lack of sensitivity or compassion
- Unforgiveness
- Emotional distance
- Faithlessness (through either emotional or physical affairs)
- Anger
- Hopelessness

Opening Your Heart to Love

You can't make another person love you, no matter how hard you try. But there's one thing you can do to help love flourish: open your heart.

You may not realize it, but there's a door to your heart that only you can open or close from the inside. This is the result of God *giving* you a free will and *respecting* you enough to allow you to exercise it at your own discretion (even when it's not always in your best interest). You actually open and close this door to your heart throughout your day as you navigate the challenges that come your way.

You wake up to a brand-new day. The sun is shining, and the birds are singing. Your heart opens up a little bit in anticipation of a good day.

You head for the kitchen, where your spouse gives you a dirty look and reminds you about your failure to take the trash out. You dutifully carry out the garbage, but inside your heart closes a little bit.

You get in the car to head for work. On the highway, an aggressive speeder cuts you off, forcing you to slam on the brakes. Blood is rapidly pumping through your body, but your heart closes down a little bit out of fear and irritation. Then later on, another driver briefly pauses, waves at you, and lets you make a left turn. Your heart opens back up just a little bit.

At work your boss praises you for the report you finished yesterday. You can feel your heart opening again as you savor that compliment for a job well done. A half hour later, a coworker accuses you of stealing a container of yogurt out of the break room refrigerator. As you return to your office, your heart closes down a little once again.

Back home later that evening, you see on the news that there has been another mass shooting at a high school. Your heart closes a bit with the sorrow of one more senseless attack, but then another report describes how one student heroically stopped the shooter, saving many lives. You're grateful, and your heart opens back up a bit more.

That's the way it goes for many of us every day. We may not realize it, but our hearts are opening and closing all the time as we confront everything that happens in our lives.

Complicating matters even more are the situations and events that hurt us or startle us enough to cause us to slam the door shut! When we do that, we hunker down in our internal fortress to avoid further hurt or devastation.

In many ways, the way we humans open and close our hearts mirrors the creative ways some of God's other creatures protect their vulnerable parts. Roly-poly bugs scrunch themselves into tight little balls when they're disturbed. Turtles retreat into their shells. Even predators such as sharks protect themselves by closing their eyes the instant before they bite into a victim. This process of opening up when things seem safe and closing down when we're afraid is completely normal and natural. That's the way God designed us.

But problems can develop when we close our hearts tight and then forget to ever open them back up again. We may not realize it, but when we close our hearts to another person, we risk shutting down the flow of God's love. He hasn't changed—God still loves us. But we've disconnected ourselves from the source. No flow.

I (Greg) had to learn about opening and closing my heart the hard way: through difficult experiences I went through with my family and with my wife, Erin.

Family Frustrations

Back in the early 2000s, I was helping my family run the Smalley Relationship Center in Branson, Missouri, when a dispute arose over my leadership. Apparently, my fellow family members did not consider me the great leader I believed myself to be, so they decided to relieve me of my duties. Making the experience even more bitter for me, they installed one of my siblings as the new leader in my place.

This was a real heart-closer for me. I felt I had been cut to the core on multiple fronts: business, ministry, and family dynamics. I didn't realize the full impact at the time, but I left this situation feeling wounded, rejected, and depressed. I had clearly lost that lovin' feelin' for my family.

I have always been better at figuring out things analytically in my brain than at sorting out the complex emotions in my heart. At one point I thought my cognitive abilities meant I should become an attorney. But at this time, as my depression grew deeper, I could see that this was one problem I would not be able to analyze myself out of.

I was really hurting. But this closed heart was feeling less like relief and more like living in a self-imposed prison. I needed someone to help me understand and reopen my heart. I realized that with some help, this was a golden opportunity to get to know myself better. Remember, I have an ongoing relationship with myself, and I want it to be a good one. I want to continually feel well cared for. As a responsible adult, here was my chance.

HEALTHY ADULT

Well Cared For:
1. Physically
2. Mentally
3. Emotionally
4. Spiritually

Boundary of
Personal
Responsibility

I asked a counselor to help me find my way. The counselor did what counselors often do. He asked me to focus on the precise thing I most wanted to avoid: previous family episodes that had left me feeling rejected, discarded, and emotionally closed.

Going down this disturbing memory lane was no fun, but I did discover something important. My counselor suggested that I focus on opening my heart to God rather than trying to force it open right then regarding my family. He didn't think I could love anybody named Smalley at that time unless God's divine love was flowing freely through me.

As I lived in that uncomfortable position and focused on trying to grasp and experience God's love for me, I was led to the passage in Peter's first epistle about the "living stone": "The stone that the builders rejected has become the cornerstone" (1 Peter 2:7). I had read this passage hundreds of times before, a passage that speaks of Christ being rejected by many but ultimately becoming the basis of a new way all people could relate to God.

This time I read it in a new light. I was reminded that rejection was a common experience in life. Obviously, there was nothing to like about my situation. However, in time, I came to see that the rejection I had experienced with my family was not fatal. In fact, it was nothing compared to the rejection Christ had endured.

So, instead of wallowing in my depression and strategizing how I could pay back offending family members, I transitioned to opening my heart to Christ. I shared my rejection with Him and asked Him to love me and heal me. As I opened my heart to God, I could feel His love flow into the empty and fearful places within me. Over time, as this internal healing continued, I could once more reach out to my family with an open heart, ready to love them and embrace them again.

This is not to suggest I just blew the whole experience off and pretended it never happened. But I didn't want the burden of carrying the unforgiveness anymore. It was okay that I curled up like a roly-poly bug when I felt my family had rejected me, but it was essential that I not remain in that defensive posture. I don't want to live that way, and I don't want to be that man! I needed to relax, open up, and allow my heart to experience God's love.

Things happen to all of us that make us want to close up our hearts. The problem is that some of us get stuck in the closed position, not realizing we have allowed our pain to make us close the door on our hearts. We still might try to have relationships with people in this closed state, but those relationships are doomed to be superficial and disposable. And maybe worse, we become a person we don't want to be.

Fight or Flight

I've had plenty of roly-poly moments during my twenty-eight years of marriage to Erin. I grew up in a family where the guys used sarcasm to connect. I know that sounds strange, but we enjoyed the banter and trying to one-up each other. This style of relating, for the most part, worked well between my dad, my brother, and me. Not surprisingly, I imported this combustible approach into my marriage to Erin. And not surprisingly, it didn't work out, especially during moments of conflict.

One evening, Erin and I were barbecuing chicken on the grill. It was a perfect summer day in Colorado, so we ate outside on the back deck as a family. And after eating an amazing dinner, Erin had to run an errand.

We had bought extra chicken breasts that were still on the counter. So before leaving the house, Erin made sure that I knew to put them away. "Don't leave the raw chicken out," Erin reminded me as she left.

I rolled my eyes, thinking, *I'm perfectly capable of cleaning up without instructions!*

The kids and I stayed outside talking and laughing. And then a spontaneous football game broke out in the backyard. After running around, we were all worn out. So we decided to relax by watching a movie. All of us simply slipped inside the basement door and lounged in front of the big TV.

It was a perfect evening of good food, fun, and relaxation. But something kept gnawing at me. It was like I was forgetting something! But I pushed the thought out of my mind and continued watching the movie.

I didn't realize that Erin had returned until I heard her shout, "Seriously!" followed by, "Get off the counter!"

Thinking that a mouse or some large insect was attacking Erin, I raced up the stairs. I entered the kitchen just in time to see Erin shooing our cat, Fiona, from the counter.

And then I remembered what I'd forgotten: the raw chicken.

I'm sure that Fiona thought she'd died, gone to heaven, and was now feasting at the Marriage Supper of the Lamb . . . only it was the supper of the chicken! Fiona had eaten her way into several of the Styrofoam packages and now looked like the fat lasagna-loving cartoon cat Garfield.

"I told you to put the chicken away before I left!" Erin yelled in frustration. "Now I have to throw all of this chicken away! And Fiona is going to get sick from eating raw meat!"

I had blown it. But instead of admitting my mistake and apologizing, I argued with Erin. *About what?* you might be wondering. I was clearly in the wrong. I had failed to put the chicken back in the freezer as Erin had requested. No argument there. Instead, I focused on the only part of her outburst that I could defend against. "Fiona isn't going to get sick," I bantered. "She's a cat. She eats raw meat every time she catches a mouse!"

Proud of my feline acumen, I smugly waited for Erin's rebuttal. But all I got back from her was a sarcastic "Really?"

We've gone through this fight-and-flight scenario more times than I care to count. The sad truth is that when my heart shuts down like that roly-poly bug, I become argumentative and sarcastic.

But I'm so grateful Erin and I have been able to address this issue in our relationship. Over twenty-eight years of marriage, we've learned how to open our hearts and work through our issues. Our upcoming discussion of the Reactive Cycle (a component of Lie #6) will help you learn how to manage and resolve conflicts in a healthy way. However, some people turn into roly-poly bugs so often, or close their hearts down so tight, that they risk becoming permanently closed to each other.

That easily could have happened to us. I never had to wonder with Erin whether she was upset with me. It was obvious. But she never really knew when I was upset with her. I might have been seething inside, but I didn't reveal that to her—except through sarcasm. That kind of guardedness can be as damaging to a marriage as being argumentative.

I've learned to make sure that other people don't control the door that opens and closes my heart. That door is my responsibility. I can close it down when I need to, but I need to open it back up if I want our love to grow. This skill has proven to be of great benefit to me and was a powerful starting point.

Don't Forget to Guard Your Heart

It takes an open heart to love God, your neighbor, and your partner. But don't let your heart become permanently stuck in the open position. That might leave you vulnerable to serious harm.

The Bible mentions the heart more than seven hundred times, and in Proverbs we are counseled to take good care of it. One version of Proverbs 4:23 says to guard your heart, because everything you do flows from it. But I think *The Message* version paraphrase is clearer: "Keep vigilant watch over your heart; *that's* where life starts."

The point Scripture makes here is simple: The heart is our Holy of Holies, our spiritual control center, the place where we experience the love of God and people. God wants us to keep our hearts open to His love and open to the love of others, but He wants us to guard our hearts against those who would mistreat or injure them. This is a critical component of responsibly caring for ourselves. We have focused here on opening closed hearts because closed hearts cut people off from God and are a major source of problems for so many couples. But don't misunderstand us to be saying that you should never close the door of your heart.

The important thing is to follow the example of the roly-poly. Know when to close up tight and know when to open back up and get on with living and loving. This becomes the essence of healthy Christ-centered boundaries.

Many people mistakenly believe that the primary goal of effective boundaries is to get someone to stop doing or saying something. That makes complete sense when that person is doing or saying something you don't like. Unfortunately, though, any attempt to guide another's behavior is either controlling or manipulative. Whether we like it or not, the result of our attempts to control or manipulate is that we have to become controlling and manipulative to succeed. Nobody likes being controlled, and nobody really likes being a manipulative person. Everybody loses!

A better alternative is instead to make the goal of the boundary creating a space for yourself that enables your heart to stay open. Let's say that your spouse gets angry when you argue. If your goal is to get your spouse to stop being angry, that is controlling. However, make your goal to care for yourself and keep your heart open. Don't say, "You better stop yelling or I'm going to leave." That is controlling. Instead say something like, "You can do what you want, but if you keep coming at me with anger, I'm going to leave. But I'll be back later so we can finish our discussion." That statement is respecting your spouse's right to be angry, while responsibly attending to your need and desire to stay open. In the end, it's not about your spouse; it's about you. It's not about judging your spouse's behavior; it's about you taking care of you.

That may seem like a small detail, but in the end it's huge! As we will continue to demonstrate throughout this book, we've come to learn a radical truth: Responsibly caring well for yourself invariably turns out to be in everyone's best interest.

Seeing Love Grow

A funny thing happens with so many of the couples we work with. They quit trying to manufacture love or manipulate their partners into providing it. Instead, they focus on opening their hearts and letting love grow.

Jon and Brittany have been doing a lot better since they quit trying to make each other love them in ways that aren't natural. Once they turned the spotlight away from the holes in their relationship and worked on staying more open so they could enjoy each other more fully, both of them began to feel more alive and more loving.

To help them keep moving in the right direction, we gave them some homework.

Heart-Opening Exercises

"If you build it, he will come." That was the advice the voice from heaven gave to the Iowa farmer in the movie *Field of Dreams.* Sure enough, the farmer built the baseball field, and soon it was filled with players.

We believe similar things can happen to your love when you

learn to open your heart. Here are some exercises to get you going and keep you growing.

1. How open is your heart to God right now? Take some time and reflect on this.

       Have you struggled in your relationship with God? How?

       Seek ways to understand Him better and experience His love for you. We know many people who have experienced breakthroughs through the spiritual disciplines of quietness, reflection, and practicing openness to God. See if you can build these practices into your life.

2. How open is your heart to your partner right now? Is the door of your heart wide open? Or is it cracked open only half an inch? Or is it closed snug

and tight, double padlocked, surrounded by barbed
wire, and patrolled by slobbering rottweilers?

3. Practice watching the door of your heart open and
close.

I (Greg) showed how I have been like the roly-poly
bug: closed when necessary but opened up again as
soon as possible. In the right circumstances, both are
responsible and both are valuable.

Monitor the door of your own heart throughout
the day.

And monitor the door of your heart as you
interact with your partner.

4. Emotions are the voices of your heart.

Learn how to pay attention to them and interpret
what your heart is saying. Each partner benefits by
learning how to go through life with both heart and
brain fully engaged. At times that will involve learning
to get in touch with the feelings in your heart. At
times that will mean working things out in your head
by asking analytical questions:

What am I feeling now?
Why am I feeling that?
And what does this feeling show me?

We realize that for some of you the idea of emotions being that important may be troubling or confusing. We've all been subject to years of unfortunate and misguided cultural training about feelings. So, when unpacking Lie #8, we'll discuss God's purpose and intent when He created feelings. If, for the moment, this idea seems too ridiculous or just too off base, park the idea to the side and wait for later to see if we can effectively demonstrate how paying attention to your feelings is an often-unseen opportunity.

5. Ask God to let you see through His eyes and feel with His heart.

This will only make sense to people who really know how to connect with God personally. Many of us believe that when we accepted Jesus as our Lord and Savior, what we did was "ask Him into our hearts." This would suggest He actually lives in us. If that is true, as we believe, it opens up an exciting option: At any moment we can ask God to let us look through His eyes to see what He sees. We can also ask Him to let us feel what He feels. Commonly, when we see what He sees and feel what He feels, the differences are striking! Then we get to decide: my view or His? My feelings or His?

Ask God to let you see your spouse through His eyes. Look for things you may have overlooked. Pay particular attention to differences between how you have seen your spouse and how He does. Ask to see what He loves and values about your spouse, and ask Him why.

Ask God to let you feel what He feels for your spouse. This one can be overwhelming. Notice that God sees it all, the good and the bad, but apparently His love and adoration is unending regardless. Ask Him to let you feel His love deeply.

Last but not least, look in the mirror and ask God to let you see yourself through His eyes. Notice the differences between what you see and what He sees. Then ask Him to let you feel what He feels for you. Compare and contrast. Then you get to choose. Will it be your view or His? Your feelings or His? In all cases, we typically like His better!

6. Enjoy engaged discussions with your partner.

Instead of talking from a distance—his corner and her corner—sit down close to each other and talk openly. Hold each other's hands. Look into each other's eyes. Learn how to "be" with each other in the moment, not distracted or preoccupied, but focused on your spouse.

LOVE LIE #4:

I MUST SACRIFICE WHO I AM FOR THE SAKE OF MY MARRIAGE

Ray and Debra enjoyed their weekend getaway, but they were exhausted when they finally got home late Sunday night. So they quickly stashed their black suitcase on the stairway landing and went upstairs to bed. On Monday morning, both returned to their normal routines.

And the suitcase remained on the landing. Neither Ray nor Debra picked it up and carried it upstairs. Soon the job of taking care of the suitcase became a battle of wills. Ray didn't want to move it—Debra was home all day, so why didn't she move it? For Ray, the situation became a symbol of who wears the pants in the family. Debra didn't want to move the suitcase either; she was busy all day with the kids and the house chores—and after all, weren't men supposed to carry suitcases?

Three weeks later the suitcase still sat on the landing.

Sound familiar? Either Ray or Debra could have easily moved the suitcase. But both of them believed doing so was the other person's responsibility. Don't ask us where people get their ideas about who should do what, but we all have them firmly planted in our heads.

A Stinky Situation

Soon it was time for Ray to leave on a business trip, and he needed the black suitcase.

But using it was impossible, because the suitcase was no longer a simple suitcase. It had long ago morphed into a big, huge (but mostly unspoken) issue! So, instead, Ray found a smaller and less suitable bag for his business trip.

But just before leaving, his passive-aggressive behavior became downright aggressive-aggressive. He went to the refrigerator, grabbed a piece of blue cheese, hid it inside the suitcase, and walked out the door.

If this mini-battle sounds familiar, it is.

Millions of us saw this struggle play out between characters Ray and Debra Barone during a favorite episode of the popular TV series *Everybody Loves Raymond*. But even people who've never seen a minute of *Everybody Loves Raymond* can recognize Ray and Debra's disagreement over what's "mine," what's "yours," and what's "ours."

Sitcoms end on happy notes, and sure enough, the appropriately titled "Baggage" episode concluded with Ray and Debra realizing the silliness of their behavior, hugging, making up, and trying to act like adults. It's a humorous way to end a TV show, but in the real world of marriage, such standoffs don't always end with hugs and laughter.

Most people view sacrifice in the same way as Ray and Debra— as surrender: give in or give up. Each refused to give in and move a suitcase for a month, which was about pride. Surrendering or giving in is truly a type of sacrifice, and the episode lasted for only half an hour. But many of the men and women we've worked with have struggled for years with unnecessary turf battles and tugs-of-war.

Some won't give an inch.

Some give in way more than they should.

Some say they've already given all and don't have anything left to give.

It's all part of the story of how suitcases become issues and molehills become mountains.

However, we really want to focus on the common underlying issue: people believing that sacrifice requires that they change who they are for the sake of their spouses, and for the sake of God. They feel a need or pressure to sacrifice themselves—who they are, what they want, how they feel—for those they love.

We typically feel that same push to adjust who we are regardless of whether we give in or resist it. However, beyond any normal societal pressure, many Christians believe that changing aspects of who we are is a central component of transforming into a more sacrificial and Christlike person.

Self-Assessment

1. How do you typically handle your turf battles as a couple? How do you experience your spouse during these tugs-of-war?

   - I/they won't give an inch.
   - I/they give in way more than I/they should.
   - I/they say I/they have already given all and don't have anything left to give.

2. In the context of marriage, what do "sacrifice" and "dying to self" mean to you? Explain.

3. In terms of sacrifice, to what degree do you feel pressure to change who you are, what you want, or how you feel for the sake of your spouse, and for the sake of God?

1	2	3	4	5	6	7	8	9	10
No Pressure				Neutral			Great Pressure		

4. Which of the following statements do you *most* connect with?

- "It feels like all I do is give, give, give."
- "I pour myself into everyone else and I've tried to be sacrificial, but there's no 'me' left anymore."
- "I feel exhausted, depleted, cheated, and dead inside."
- "I feel like unless I give up me and change who I am for my spouse, he/she will never be satisfied."
- "I don't even know who I am anymore—what I want or how I feel."
- "Other people matter more than I do."

His, Hers, or Ours

Talking to couples about love and sacrifice in marriage can be complicated. Some seem to have worked out relationships of easygoing reciprocity. But notice that the conversation often remains on the surface, discussing sacrifice primarily in terms of who does what, and how much each gives:

"Sure, I give 100 percent, but so does my partner. I guess that adds up to 200 percent!"

Others tell us they've experienced more than their share of "suitcase" episodes and other immovable objects in their marriage. They're tired of seeing nonevents turn into big deals. They feel pressured to act, to take the first step, to sacrifice whatever pride that keeps them from moving closer, but a deep-seated resentment stops them.

It feels like all I do is give, give, give.

I pour myself into everyone else, drip after drip after drip, until I feel like there is no "me" left anymore.

I feel exhausted, depleted, cheated, and dead inside.

However, through the power struggles, many also connect to the deeper levels of frustration and say things like, "I feel like unless I give up me and change who I am for my spouse, he/she will never be satisfied."

When we talk to men to help them figure out how they get stuck in conflict with their wives, many of them sound just like Ray Barone.

"My wife doesn't really appreciate how demanding and draining my job is."

"She doesn't see that I give 110 percent at work and 110 percent at home."

"She wants me to change and be more like her."

Talk to twenty-first-century men and you'll hear a story of frustration and even anger about how their wives don't appreciate or acknowledge all they are doing, and how fundamentally different they are from their wives. Many husbands say they have made serious efforts to commit more time to children and housework, but they don't feel like anyone has noticed. They don't really feel appreciated for who they are as a person, and for who they are as a man.

When we talk to wives about where they get stuck, echoes of Debra Barone are unmistakable.

"My husband doesn't really appreciate how demanding it is to do everything for the kids and for the house."

"He doesn't see how much I give, give, and give until there's nothing left to give, until there's nothing left of me."

"I work full-time too. Why's it always all about him?"

"He wants me to be more like him and to do things how he wants them done."

"He complains about me being too emotional and tries to get me to be more 'rational,' like him."

We realize that some of the above comments reference numerous gender stereotypes, and we understand that roles and responsibilities today are very fluid. We are using them here primarily because those stereotypes still exist, and there are still many couples who relate to them. Please notice, though, that the bigger issue we want to address regards the pressure you might feel to be different somehow, and to sacrifice or change who you are.

Giving Until It Hurts

There are couples who engage in monthlong standoffs, like Ray and Debra. But in many cases, one partner gives in more readily than the other. Some even embrace giving in as their main purpose in marriage.

A woman named Sandra compared her lifetime of marital sacrifice to Christ's sacrifice of His life on the cross. "Sacrifice is what Jesus did," Sandra said. "It's what a Christian does. It's what a spouse does. For me, wearing a wedding ring is like carrying a cross. I do it all for them. I must die to myself."

Only twice in the entire Bible are we told to do something

every day. Hebrews 3:13 says we are to "encourage one another day after day" (NASB), and Luke 9:23 says believers are to take up their cross daily.

So isn't sacrificing yourself—who you are, what you want, how you feel, for those you love and for God—what a loving spouse and faithful follower of Christ does? After all, sacrifice *is* a main theme in the Bible:

For God so loved the world, that he gave his only Son.
JOHN 3:16

Greater love has no one than this, that someone lay down his life for his friends.
JOHN 15:13

Therefore be imitators of God, as beloved children. And walk in love, as Christ loved us and gave himself up for us, a fragrant offering and sacrifice to God.
EPHESIANS 5:1-2

By this we know love, that he [Jesus Christ] laid down his life for us, and we ought to lay down our lives for the brothers.
I JOHN 3:16

But God shows his love for us in that while we were still sinners, Christ died for us.
ROMANS 5:8

In this is love, not that we have loved God but that he loved us and sent his Son to be the propitiation for our sins.
I JOHN 4:10

And the life I now live in the flesh I live by faith in the
Son of God, who loved me and gave himself for me.

GALATIANS 2:20

The truth is that we are called to sacrifice. The lie, however, is a
twisting of the truth. And that distortion leads to an unfortunate
sequence of beliefs and behaviors: People often mistakenly interpret "die to self" and "carry my cross" to mean that they need to
see others as more important than they are, as fundamentally of
greater value. Thus, people think that because of their worthlessness
outside of Christ, they need to continually sacrifice—to keep giving
regardless of their well-being and regardless of how much it hurts.

Somehow, the result of all of that is supposed to bless the Lord
and bless others. But as we've already shown, the common results
lead to statements like these:

- "I've tried to be faithful and sacrificial, but there's no 'me'
  left."
- "I don't even know who I am anymore, what I want, how
  I feel."
- "I feel dead inside."
- "I'm exhausted."
- "I feel cheated."

While we appreciate Sandra's commitment, we don't really believe
God designed marriage to be a means of torture and death. You
can't have a great marriage without sacrifice, but if you miss the
true essence of what God is actually calling us to, you end up sacrificing too much of yourself.

So how did Sandra convince herself that marriage is a form of
crucifixion? These were her thoughts:

1. *God gave His son for us.* John 3:16, one of the most popular verses in the Bible, spells out this loving sacrifice: "For God so loved the world, that he gave his only Son, that whoever believes in him should not perish but have eternal life."

2. *We should give our lives for Him and for others.* Christ's sacrifice on the cross is unique, but it provides a model for how we should love each other sacrificially: "By this we know love, that he laid down his life for us, and we ought to lay down our lives for the brothers" (1 John 3:16).

3. *Other people matter more than I do.* The previous two statements are rock-solid biblical truths. Sandra's third idea comes from her own history and life experience, and it worries us. It reflects a common next step in the thought process. There's a fine line between true humility and its counterfeits: self-doubt, self-loathing, and/or self-betrayal.

4. *I must sacrifice (change/alter) who I am for the sake of our marriage.* Paul pleaded with followers of Christ to walk in humility: "Do nothing from selfish ambition or conceit, but in humility count others more significant than yourselves" (Philippians 2:3). It all makes sense, doesn't it? Can you see how easy it is to follow this line of thinking? But Paul wasn't talking about Sandra and her husband. Philippians 2:3 is not a teaching on marriage, a topic that Paul addresses in other letters. Paul is urging believers to respect their fellow brothers and sisters as equals rather than promoting themselves.

Let's dive into this thought sequence a little deeper to see if we can unravel the mess and better set ourselves up to succeed, personally and relationally.

First, we need to provide a little context. Remember for a moment that the author of lies is our mortal Enemy, Satan. His purposes are to steal, kill, and destroy, while in contrast Jesus came for us to have life to the full (see John 10:10). Satan's goal is to tear us down in order to render us ineffective. Jesus' intent is to build us up in Him in order to fully empower us.

The battle between the two is real, and we already know who wins in the end. However, if Satan can twist the truth in our minds, causing us to operate outside of the Lord's design and protection, the Enemy can destroy us as individuals. He may not ultimately win the war, but he wins the battle for our souls. He picks us off one at a time.

What Is Godly Sacrifice?

Todd is a commercial pilot. He travels for several days at a time. He's exhausted from traveling, staying in hotel rooms, eating room service, and dealing with grumpy passengers. When he finally gets home, he finds his wife, Becky, also exhausted from taking care of their two young children, working as a photographer, and managing the household responsibilities. When he walks in the door, Becky hands off the children.

"Dinner is in the Crock-Pot," she hastily says. "I need a break. I'm going out with my girlfriends."

Todd begins to object, but he doesn't want to start a fight. They've had the "who is more tired" battle before, and it's such a waste of time.

However, on a deeper level, Todd is a pleaser and feels guilty when his wife is unhappy. So he suppresses his needs and places Becky's desires first—he becomes a martyr. He reasons that it's his role as a husband to love his wife "as Christ loved the church" (Ephesians 5:25). And since Christ sacrificed His life for the church, Todd believes it's his job to sacrifice for Becky.

The problem is, Todd has nothing to give. He's exhausted and running on empty. He has nothing to invest in his kids or his wife. But he keeps on giving, and the loss of personal resources is stressful. However, suppressing his needs is backfiring. Resentment builds toward his wife and kids. He stuffs his emotions and reasons that this is what it means to be a husband—even if it's at the cost of his well-being. This pattern repeats itself most every time he returns from traveling.

What Todd is giving is not godly sacrifice. Yes, sacrifice is an essential daily part of Christian life, but it's meant to be an *investment* of your time, energy, love, resources—not a sacrifice of who you are. That is actually self-betrayal! Our definition of sacrifice is this: the act of giving up something of value you own—your time, money, possessions, comfort, desire, sleep, life, etc.—for the sake of someone else.

Clearly there are many of us who are like Todd and don't understand the value of who we are as individuals and what we have been given. (Our previously stated issue with the unity candle is directly related.) We are people of incalculable eternal worth and value.

Additionally, we aren't here by accident. Each one of us was intentionally placed here for a reason. God has a desire for each of us to be directly engaged with Him in His unfolding plan and purpose. Every aspect of our lives matters.

Thus, as people designed by the very hand of God, He values us to the degree He sent Jesus to die for us rather than lose us. To suppress the light within us grossly undervalues the significance of that eternal life. We may sacrifice our life for another, as Jesus did, but what makes that sacrifice so amazing is how much our life in Christ is actually worth!

Therefore, we have high value as individual people and are as valuable and important as everyone else. When we give and sacrifice something we have, the significance of the gift is directly correlated to its value.

Ideally, sacrificial love flows from a state of life-giving abundance, not from emptiness. In our possession are numerous valuable assets, our lives included. The primary responsibility we now bear becomes one of stewardship, which is simply how skillfully we manage the resources we've been entrusted with.

With that in mind, let's pause a moment and talk about stewardship in general. Once we've explained what we mean by stewardship, we'll show you how good stewardship relates to sacrifice and can contribute to making your marriage one you both love.

Components of Good Stewardship

First Peter 4:10 says, "As each of you has received a gift, use it to serve one another, as good stewards of God's varied grace." Here are three key elements of effective stewardship:

1. Value the Asset

The first essential step in good stewardship is to recognize the genuine worth and value of what has been entrusted to your care: in this case you, your life, and all you've been given. This includes your gifts and talents, your energy, and your potential to make a positive difference in your spouse's life and your family, community, world, and the kingdom of God. All of the above and more have enormous value. Please note the true value of something you possess is not only determined by what you *think* it's worth.

Imagine you are a child and know that money has value and can buy stuff, but you don't yet fully understand it. As you're walking down the street, you see a piece of paper money in the gutter. When you pick it up, it has a picture of a man and under it is the name "Franklin." In each corner is the number 100, but you don't know what any of that means. All you know is that it can buy stuff and you're excited.

So you take it to the convenience store on the corner, and on the counter you see a basket with delicious-looking individually wrapped pieces of bubble gum with a sign that says "5 cents each." You love gum, so you take a piece and ask the guy at the counter if you can buy it with *this*, as you hold out the bill. He smiles and says, "You sure can!"

You hand him the bill, and he turns to get change, but you don't know you have change coming—so you turn and happily walk out of the store. You may even be completely content with your purchase, but just because you think the $100 bill is worth a piece of bubble gum doesn't mean that's its true value.

As silly as this example may seem, sadly, we see this scenario play out with an amazing number of people we work with. They have no real idea of how much they're worth or the real value of the assets and potential that God has created in them. That they only think they're worth a piece of gum has no real bearing on their true worth. Our ultimate worth and value is determined by God alone. We actually have little say over it.

So our first responsibility of stewardship is to learn to appropriately assess and accurately value all that the Lord has entrusted us with.

2. Manage the Asset

Once you realize the value of what you have in your possession, you now have the responsibility to care for it; otherwise, through neglect or carelessness, it will lose value. For example, imagine you were given a classic car in perfect condition, worth thousands of dollars. If you don't take care of it over time, the car will develop problems. If you are reckless and the car is abused, it loses value.

Dents, scratches, tears, and unattended mechanical problems all impact its worth. But even if the vehicle is simply ignored and left in the garage, problems develop since cars need to be run in order to stay healthy, and it loses value as it sits and declines.

However, those of us who understand business and finance also know that if something has value and it's left unattended and unused, another value is lost: its potential. We see this in Jesus' parable of the talents found in Matthew 25. We understand that in those days a "talent" was a measure of money, but for our purposes we'll allow the English use of the word to help us make our point.

> For it will be as when a man going on a journey called his servants and entrusted to them his property; to one he gave five talents, to another two, to another one, to each according to his ability. Then he went away. He who had received the five talents went at once and traded with them; and he made five talents more. So also, he who had the two talents made two talents more. But he who had received the one talent went and dug in the ground and hid his master's money. Now after a long time the master of those servants came and settled accounts with them. And he who had received the five talents came forward, bringing five talents more, saying, "Master, you delivered to me five talents; here, I have made five talents more." His master said to him, "Well done, good and faithful servant; you have been faithful over a little, I will set you over much; enter into the joy of your master." And he also who had the two talents came forward, saying, "Master, you delivered to me two talents; here I have made two talents more." His master said to him, "Well done, good and faithful servant; you

have been faithful over a little, I will set you over much; enter into the joy of your master." He also who had received the one talent came forward, saying, "Master, I knew you to be a hard man, reaping where you did not sow, and gathering where you did not winnow; so I was afraid, and I went and hid your talent in the ground. Here you have what is yours." But his master answered him, "You wicked and slothful servant! You knew that I reap where I have not sowed, and gather where I have not winnowed? Then you ought to have invested my money with the bankers, and at my coming I should have received what was my own with interest. So take the talent from him, and give it to him who has the ten talents. For to every one who has will more be given, and he will have abundance; but from him who has not, even what he has will be taken away. And cast the worthless servant into the outer darkness; there men will weep and gnash their teeth."

MATTHEW 25:14-30, RSV

Hopefully, it's not hard to see here that the problem with the servant who buried his talent was that he had a valuable asset that had potential to grow and be used in more ways to bless others and further God's purpose. The lack of stewardship was the wasted potential.

The last aspect of management we want to highlight here is the importance of replenishing the assets that are renewable. As a living and breathing person of value, we have various needs to attend to. We are energy-making machines, and everything we do requires an expenditure of energy. To maintain health and vitality we need adequate rest, nutrition, exercise, and other care in order to refuel and recharge. If we allow our battery to fully discharge without a recharge, we become useless to ourselves, to others, and to God.

In our current society, as in most cultures, money is required for almost everything. If we allow our bank account to empty and do nothing to redeposit into our account, we have nothing left to use or give. We become bankrupt. This may seem like an obvious principle. Unfortunately, the vast majority of people we see don't fully understand this concept. They don't adequately attend to their whole beings—physically, mentally, emotionally, or spiritually. They may responsibly handle one area, but not all of them.

For instance, perhaps a guy maintains an active spiritual life but ignores his health. He's spiritually full but physically bankrupt. Or a gal stays physically fit but ignores her heart. Her body is in great shape, but she's an emotional wreck. In each case of poor management and neglect we suffer, our usefulness is diminished, and our purpose, at least in part, goes unfulfilled.

These are all examples of poor management of assets, and the opposite is obvious.

3. Wisely Invest the Asset

As is also clear in the parable above, God is expecting us to prudently invest all that He has given us. It's easy to think that all we possess is ours to do with as we please. But the two of us, of course, see that very differently. Everything was created by God, so in essence He owns it all. But let's take it even one step further. He already owns us, but He purchased us again when He gave His life for us. In reality, nothing we "own" is ours alone. That includes our bodies and our lives. It's all His. We often forget that major fact.

The Lord is obviously expecting us to value, manage, and *invest* all that has been entrusted to our care. As a loving Father, He

certainly wants us to be blessed, and He consistently and generously gives to us. This includes the lives we live and the very breath
we take. But it's never meant to stop there.

We are blessed to be a blessing. He remains consistently busy
unfolding His plan and purpose, and He wants us to be actively
involved with Him. But it is His plan and purpose that really
matters, not ours independent of Him. In the end, participating with God in His plan is what fulfills our purpose. In fact,
it's the only thing that makes anything in this crazy world make
any real sense!

Therefore, what we believe God is calling us to, and what we
are advocating, is learning how to fully be who you were created to
be, manage well all that you possess, and generously and effectively
allow God to guide you in the ongoing investment of what you
have been given.

Sacrifice as Investment

We're hoping you can easily see that in order for you and your
marriage to thrive, it's essential to value and manage yourself well
in all areas of life. You are valuable, and all aspects of you matter.
We will discuss in the next chapter more about how to become
and stay full, whole, and healthy.

However, in keeping with the scripturally significant theme
of sacrifice, we want to spend some time applying this essential
idea toward also investing in your spouse and your relationship.
When you make this commitment in marriage, in addition to
yourself, you now add at least two new valuable assets requiring
stewardship and investment. The first is your spouse, and the
second is your marriage. We say *at least* two, because as you add
children, they clearly become part of the equation. But for our
purposes here we'll keep it simple and just talk about spouse and
relationship.

HEALTHY MARRIAGE MODEL

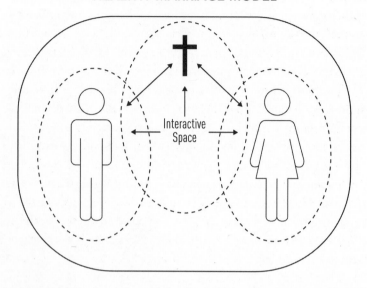

Remember, in our model of a healthy marriage, you, your spouse, and your marriage are hopefully characterized by ongoing learning and growing. A great marriage includes two imperfect people on an ongoing journey together to become more fully who they were created to be, and a relationship they create together to support those objectives. All three need continual investment and care.

When we marry, we become partners in this life journey together. We take on new responsibilities to contribute to God's Kingdom by investing significantly in the life of another.

Your spouse is God's son or daughter, whom He deeply loves. He or she was also placed on this earth with a plan and purpose. Now, in addition to discovering all we personally were placed here to become and to do, we have a sacred charge to value, encourage, support, and assist our spouse in doing the same.

As Erin and I (Greg) have journeyed together, we've gone

through numerous life stages. I've always had an outside job because it was clear that the Lord was calling me there, but I've also been involved in numerous other activities, causes, and hobbies, plus doing my part to help manage the family. Erin has, at different times, been the primary caregiver for the kids, but she has also been a nurse, gone back to school, become a counselor, and been involved with charities and causes, in addition to all the things she does for fun that charge up her battery.

Both of us are living, growing, learning, and doing plenty. Both of us matter to me. I'm as committed to supporting and encouraging her development and journey as I am to my own. In fact, I regularly choose to put aside something I might prefer to do with my time in order to make it possible for Erin to do her thing. I make a sacrificial investment in Erin. I do so willingly and joyfully (most of the time), because she and her journey are important to me too.

Sometimes I dig down and find the energy to invest in helping her with what she is doing because she and her life have real value. When I make an investment in her, I'm contributing to someone of eternal value whose life adds something important to what God is doing. In those moments I'm not actually choosing her over me, as if she and her life were *more* important than me and mine. I'm merely saying that she and her journey are *as* important as me and my journey, and thus both warrant a constant investment of our resources.

As a spiritual sidenote, we've noticed that one of the Enemy's favorite strategies is to divide and conquer. He likes to encourage us to view things in our marriage as a choice between me and you, as if one wins and the other loses, one gets his or her way and the other doesn't, one matters more than the other (remember Todd, the commercial pilot). These days we refuse to take the bait. We've come to realize that if you choose, you lose! When I sacrifice for Erin, I'm not choosing her *over* me. Instead, I'm choosing to invest something valuable of mine into something of equal and incredible value—my wife and her life! It requires a sacrifice, just as any expenditure does, but it's an investment that yields benefit to all involved.

Frequently this process of investing requires prayerful thought, and even negotiation. In chapter 9, we'll being sharing with you the Seven Steps to a Win-Win. This is a simple process to assure that both valuable people are fully accounted for at all times throughout their journey together and that neither is in any way compromised or devalued.

So in addition to investing in your spouse, we want to also focus on the investment in your relationship. Obviously, the marriage doesn't exist apart from the people in it. The people are the eternal parts and, therefore, are critical to protect and invest in. But the relationship is valuable too. In fact, when skillfully attended to, the marriage is able to greatly support and enhance the people in it.

HEALTHY MARRIAGE MODEL

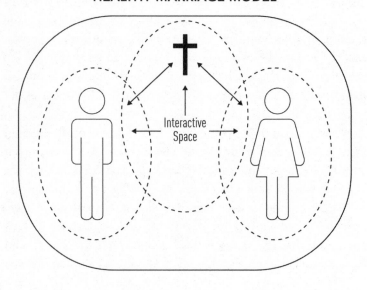

Interactive Space

Remember, the purpose of our commitment and promise (the outer circle) is to contribute to creating a safe and secure environment that allows us to relax and more fully engage together. The more confident we are that we can count on our spouse to "never leave nor forsake us," the freer we feel to be all we can be, to know and be known, and when necessary, to face the areas within that need healing and growth. So every investment we make in creating and maintaining our covenant adds something important to both our personal and marital journeys.

Those investments include all the various things we do to remain faithful and true to our marriage and family. They also include investments of time and energy to make sure our relationships get regular attention and maintenance—time taken to keep the marriage alive and well, and time to address challenges and problems. Also, hopefully, we invest time and energy into activities that create occasions of adventure and play, as well as ones of rich meaning and purpose, plus much more. And finally, to keep our marriages strong, we make investments to assure that when our spouses reach out, they generally experience us to be there with them and for them—to be the intimate friend they can truly count on.

We realize that some of you reading this book have experienced betrayal, either as the betrayer, the one betrayed, or both. The outer circle was broken. Sadly, there is nothing we deal with more commonly at our intensives than infidelity. And as painful and devastating as all of that is, we want to at least offer a word of encouragement here. Understanding that the purpose of the marriage vows is to create an extra layer of security can actually contribute to the healing and repair of a marriage. Security is created when couples reaffirm their lifelong commitment to each other. When people feel safe and secure, their hearts open and they connect and can deal with whatever problems contributed to their marriage challenges. But healing from their problems and repairing whatever damage they've caused will only happen if they feel safe and secure in a lifelong commitment.

We have witnessed God work with countless couples to rebuild a broken trust and a broken marriage. It seems to help when both spouses clearly see that the healing work is to re-create a safe environment that allows each person *and* the marriage to heal, grow, and thrive.

And you and your marriage can continue to grow and thrive when you invest in the inner circle, where the actual interaction occurs. The outer circle creates a relational "cocoon" of sorts, but the inner circle is where heart touches heart, mind engages mind, spirit joins spirit, and flesh touches flesh. Intentional investment here pays big dividends. This is where getting to know each other in deeper and deeper ways actually happens.

The inner circle is the scene of all intimate encounters. So if you want your experience to be one you both look forward to and enjoy, we can't stress enough how profitable it is to invest in creating a space you *both* love. Sometimes we like to talk about it as if it is your "home." You get to decide how it's decorated, how the house is kept, and what the tone or atmosphere is like. The key is to work (invest) together to assure that both of you are comfortable and excited to go there.

For example, when emotional issues get triggered between Erin and me, Erin prefers to talk about it immediately and deeply. She wants our intimate space to be fully open with no unresolved issues hanging around. I hate conflict, so I prefer to mull things over for a while, and if we talk about it at all, I want to ease into it. If Erin consistently tries to force me to engage her preferred way, without paying attention to my feelings and preferences, even if she succeeds and I engage, how comfortable will it be for me? Not much! How excited will I be to go there again? Not very! If she keeps pushing her way, without attention to me, she'll eventually either find herself alone there, or always have an unexcited, uncooperative partner in that space.

The alternative is to work together to create a space both enjoy being in. That will likely require an investment of time, energy, and creativity. Paying attention to how the space feels for each, what kinds of interactions feel good to both, how to handle tension, and so on, are worth discussing. Our upcoming discussion of the Seven Steps to Win-Win will help here too, and the benefits of both enjoying and looking forward to spending time in that space are well worth the effort.

A Perfect Picture of Sacrifice

Sometimes we therapists feel that we need to make everything complicated when it's really simple. Love requires sacrifice, but sacrifice doesn't require burning out the lover. A sacrifice can be as simple as a generous gift of something nice we have in order to bless another.

I (Greg) witnessed a perfect example of loving sacrifice the other day at our breakfast table. By the time our daughter Annie got to breakfast, there were three pieces of bacon left. Normally she is a complete baconaholic who could easily scarf down all three strips.

There was just one problem. Our daughter Murphy was on her way to the table, and she had a fondness for bacon too.

Annie quickly gulped down one of the warm strips of bacon. Now she was holding the remaining two pieces in her hands. We saw an interesting look pass over her face as if she was wrestling with something. Then, in one of those amazing moments that happen naturally without any parental string-pulling, Annie handed one of the pieces of bacon to Murphy.

"Hey, Dad, did you see that?" Annie asked me. "I just laid down my life for Murphy."

I gave her a big hug for connecting the dots between a Bible study the family had done and the issue of food distribution at the breakfast table. Of course, as the family wise guy I did remind her that her sacrifice wasn't as great as the pig's!

Annie's spontaneous moment of loving sacrifice provides a powerful picture of the way love works. Investments of love can be as simple as a warm hug, a knowing wink, a gentle smile, an encouraging word, sharing a piece of bacon with someone you love, or making your bed in the morning.

Wait. What? Making your bed?

Picture this: It's a bright sunny morning. As you elegantly roll out of bed and into your most comfy slippers, you lovingly glance across the rumpled duvet cover at your spouse, standing on the other side. And then you joyfully make the bed together.

I can't think of a more awful image!

I don't care about feng shui, that making your bed has its own national holiday (September 11), how a clean sleep environment is good for my health, the importance of starting the day off right, or that my mother would cringe if the bed were a mess: I hate making our bed.

Many people don't make their beds because they got up late and are behind schedule. That's not me. I like margin in the morning. I'm typically not frantically running out the door, so I can't use that as an excuse. Simply put, I like to get into a messy bed. How I rolled out of bed is how I want to climb back into bed.

Comedian Jim Gaffigan sums up my thoughts perfectly: "My wife always asks me why I don't make the bed. And I respond with the same reason why I don't tie my shoes after I take them off."[1]

Erin and I have had this argument many times throughout our twenty-seven years of marriage. I've tried to convince her that unless she's conducting tours of our bedroom while I'm away, no one will know that the bed is unmade. No dice. I've tried to explain that the idea of slipping my feet into tightly tucked sheets at night gives me the heebie-jeebies. I've even tried arguing: "I'm just going to get back in it tonight. So what's the point?" or "A messy bed allows me to get into bed faster at night." I've tried letting science prove my point by showing her a recent scientific study about the health benefits of an unmade bed, which states: "If you immediately make your bed with the sunrise, the tight sheets will trap millions of dust mites that live on your bed, feeding off your dead skin cells and sweat and potentially contributing to asthma and allergy problems. An unmade and open bed, however, exposes the creatures to fresh air and light and will help dehydrate and kill them off."[2] The fact that we have piranha-like dust mites in our bed feeding on Erin's body should have ended our long-term debate, and yet, she still wants the bed made. I'm not even going to mention the twenty pillows that grace our bed!

However, something drastically changed a few months ago—and no, I didn't finally wear Erin down. I started making the bed. You might be dumbfounded and may be asking yourself *why?*

Recently, Erin had a terrible case of plantar fasciitis (heel pain). After going through treatment, she ended up in a protective boot. She wasn't supposed to put any weight on her injured foot for several weeks and looked so pitiful hopping around the house on her crutches.

The first morning after she was placed in her boot, I found Erin circling our bed while hopping on one foot.

"Are you serious!" I scolded her. "You're making the bed with only one good foot! Let it go. Making the bed is not worth injuring yourself!"

"I know it doesn't make sense to you," Erin explained, "but I really like our bed made. It makes me feel good."

And finally, after decades of marriage, I understood how important making the bed was to my wife. Sadly, it took Erin almost reinjuring her foot to cause me to see the light, but I finally got it. More importantly, I realized that this was an opportunity to sacrifice a little bit of my time in the morning for my wife—to make a sacrificial investment in her.

Sacrifice Exercises

Valuing Yourself

Satan (the father of lies) wants you to believe that other people matter more than you. God's truth says that you are of incalculable worth and value. He sent His Son to die for you. That's how much God values you! God sees your worth, but do you? Reflect on these verses and allow God's truth about you to be written on your heart:

> So God created man in his own image, in the image of God he created him; male and female he created them.
> GENESIS 1:27

> I am fearfully and wonderfully made.
> PSALM 139:14

> You shall be my treasured possession.
> EXODUS 19:5

> You are my glorious inheritance.
> SEE EPHESIANS 1:18

> Because you are precious in my eyes . . .
> ISAIAH 43:4

> Anyone who harms you harms my most precious possession.
> SEE ZECHARIAH 2:8

> Look at the birds of the air: they neither sow nor reap nor gather into barns, and yet your heavenly Father feeds them. Are you not of more value than they?
>
> MATTHEW 6:26

> For we are God's masterpiece. He has created us anew in Christ Jesus.
>
> EPHESIANS 2:10, NLT

What do these verses say about your value and worth in God's eyes? You have high value as a person, and you are as valuable and important as everyone else. Remember, everything you have been given and now possess has value. When you sacrifice something you have, the significance of the gift is directly correlated to the value of it.

Caring for Your Value

Once you realize the value of what you have in your possession, you now have the responsibility to care for it; otherwise through neglect or carelessness it will lose value. The key is to attend to your whole being—physical, mental, emotional, and spiritual. Remember, you can't give what you don't have!

List one specific way that you will take better care of yourself over the next month in each of these four areas:

Spiritual:

Physical:

Emotional:

Mental:

Blessed to Be a Blessing

God expects you to value, manage, and *invest* all that has been entrusted to your care. As a loving Father, He certainly wants you to be blessed, and He is consistently and generously giving to you. An important part of being a blessing to your spouse is through *sacrifice*. Godly sacrifice is the daily *investment* of something you own and value—your time, money, energy, possessions, comfort, sleep, desire, resources—for the sake of your spouse. You aren't sacrificing who you are; instead, you are outdoing your spouse in showing honor (Romans 12:10).

Over the next few weeks, look for specific ways you can sacrifice for and invest in your spouse. For example, you could:

- sacrifice your time: run an errand when you really want to be home, work an extra job to pay off debt, cook dinner when you're tired, cancel what you wanted to do to assist your spouse, or make the bed

- sacrifice your money: buy your spouse something with money you've saved for your hobby, use vacation dollars to visit your in-laws, use discretionary income so your spouse can go on a trip with friends

- sacrifice your sleep: get up in the middle of the night for a crying child, deal with the kids so your spouse can nap, stay up late to help your spouse with his or her project

A Space You Both Enjoy

Remember that the inner circle of the Healthy Marriage Model is where intimate encounters take place. So if you want your experience to be one you both look forward to and enjoy, it's critical to invest time in creating a space you *both* love. Ask your spouse the following questions as a way to strengthen your relationship:

- What makes you feel secure and safe?
- How can I best support you when you're having a bad day or feeling blue?
- Are there any talents, skills, or hobbies that you would like to develop? How could I help make that a reality?
- What kinds of gifts do you most enjoy getting from me?
- How do you best like to be cared for when you get sick?
- How could we strengthen our spiritual intimacy together?
- Is there anything you'd like to accomplish before you die?
- What are three goals you have for this year?
- What are your top ten goals for your lifetime?
- How could we better celebrate holidays?
- How could our sex life become even better? In our current season of life, how often would you like to have sex? What is your favorite foreplay activity to turn you on?
- Do you prefer to spend most weekends lazing around the house, getting out of the house, or being productive?
- What are some activities that we could do together (TV, movies, sports, hiking, walking, baking, dancing, concerts, theater, shopping, coffee, board or card games)?
- After we put the kids down for bed, describe your ideal way we would spend the evening.
- What rituals could be added to our relationship on a daily, weekly, monthly, and yearly basis that would help us to remain close?
- What are some things I've done for you that really made you feel loved?
- In what ways do you like to be romanced?
- What one topic do you wish I would be able to talk about more openly and freely?
- What are your career goals one, five, and twenty years from now?

- What do you think is the secret behind couples that have been happily married for more than thirty years?
- What mistakes have you seen in other couples that you want to make sure don't happen in our marriage?
- What do you think is the best relationship advice you've ever received?

LOVE LIE #5:

YOU MUST MEET EACH OTHER'S NEEDS

All her life Ashley strived to meet the high expectations of her parents, partners in a successful law firm, and measure up to her two older sisters, Pam and Brittany, who were both straight-A students, popular, and beautiful.

"So many times, we would all be sitting around the dinner table, and praises spilled out all over Pam and Brittany," Ashley told Ryan when they had been dating awhile. "I'd hear those praises and then receive my parents' comments on my own grades, social actions, immature behavior." From then on, Ashley kept playing those comments over and over in her brain:

If you would only try harder.
Learn to be disciplined.
Don't be so emotional.
Stop crying.
Grow up!

"Typically, after hearing one discouraging remark after another, I'd go to my room, close the door, and sob. No one came to offer a soft word, a hug, or to ask me how I felt. I'd ask myself what I could do to make my parents really care about me. I was trying as hard as I knew how to, and it wasn't ever enough. When I would stop crying and go back downstairs, it seemed that no one even noticed that I'd been gone."

Sometimes the pain and loneliness lasted long after Ashley's tears had stopped. At other times she fantasized about a bright future. Down deep, she knew she was a good person. At the very least, she was full of raw potential and had tons of love to give. She knew if she just found the right guy, who really loved her as much as she loved him, everything would be great. When she found Mr. Right, she was determined to be his Mrs. Right.

In her search for her ideal candidate, Ashley believed his most important quality would be his desire to please her, praise her, and fill up the dark places in her soul where longing lived unfulfilled. He would see what her parents had ignored: a loving little girl who was more than the grades she didn't get or the strong emotions she showed. Gone would be the days of crying alone in her bedroom.

She wisely knew he would have needs of his own, too, maybe even his own hurts and disappointments from his past. But that was okay, because she had loads of love to give. She was understanding and compassionate and prepared to do everything in her power to be the woman of his dreams. She was determined to love so thoroughly that he'd be a fool to think he could ever be loved any better. With a willing attitude like that, how could she miss?

When she met Ryan, it didn't take long for her to know that she'd found her guy. He was kind and caring yet still had a strong, masculine quality. And best of all, he really seemed to love her!

He even paid attention to the little things, like remembering how much she loved daffodils, hiding little love notes in unexpected places for her, and sending random text messages just to say he was thinking of her.

Their marriage ceremony was perfect too. At just the right moment the pastor looked at Ryan and said, "Young man, you have clearly been blessed to have found such a beautiful and loving young woman. She, like all women, has various wants and needs. Now, as you become her husband, you have both an opportunity and a sacred responsibility before the Lord to faithfully strive to identify those needs, and do everything in your power to meet them."

He followed by turning to Ashley and saying, "And, young lady, in a similar way, this fine young man also has wants and needs of his own. Now, as his wife you have both an opportunity and responsibility to become aware of those needs and desires, and do all in your power to meet them." Those words were music to her ears. She was already way ahead of him on that one.

He concluded that portion by adding, "As the two of you carefully and attentively love each other in that way, you will surely bless each other, and in so doing, bless the Lord."

After the wedding and a wonderful honeymoon, Ryan and Ashley settled into a comfortable town house near Ryan's job with an engineering firm. Their new home was just a few blocks away from the elementary school where Ashley taught third grade. They periodically went to church and joined a couples' Bible study. Life was full and seemed to be meeting Ashley's hopes and expectations.

Within a year, though, some other feelings began to arise. Ryan was really focused on building his career and was often distracted. He didn't hide love notes for her anymore, and he only occasionally sent her a text that wasn't about what they were having for dinner or if she remembered to do some chore. Disappointment became an increasingly common companion, and discontentment gnawed at her. Suspicion set up camp in her mind, and some of the fears from her past crept in. She even began to question herself about Ryan's feelings toward her.

Does he love me as much as he says he does?

Why doesn't he ask me about my feelings like he used to?

Was he really working late, or was he having a drink with a woman at work?

Did he seem interested in our sexy neighbor at the barbecue last week?

Pretty soon Ashley didn't just ask herself these questions. She started asking Ryan. He tried to assure her he still loved her as much as ever, apologized for not asking about her feelings, swore he was working late and not with a coworker, and laughed at the idea of being interested in their neighbor. He pulled Ashley into a strong hug and whispered more words of assurance. She breathed deeply and relaxed into his embrace. The old feelings retreated into their cocoon.

But Ashley's displeasure grew worse instead of better. When Ryan's increased efforts to please Ashley failed, he became more and more frustrated. He started to stay out late and look for relief from the pressure at home. He wasn't having an affair, but he knew his late evenings with some of the guys at work really worried Ashley. Ryan reasoned that when he was home, the well of what felt like neediness seemed bottomless. She always needed more: more compliments, more reassurance, more time with him, more, more, more. Ryan gave up trying so hard.

Fights became a nightly occurrence. Raised voices and untrue accusations were hurled across the distance between Ryan and

Ashley. He fought back for a number of months. He prayed, talked to friends, read books. He withdrew emotionally but still tried to be physically present with Ashley. He knew how much she hated to be left alone with her escalating emotions, but his own needs were screaming for attention too.

"You are *not* meeting my needs!" Ashley yelled at Ryan again, one night after a tense dinner.

Ryan stormed out of the house without a word. All Ashley heard was the garage door going up and Ryan's car speeding off. Alone in his car, Ryan asked himself, *Why is it always all about her needs and her wants? What about me?*

Meanwhile, fear and panic seized Ashley. Ryan had never left her alone before. He had always been patient, loving, and reassuring. Old, negative feelings overwhelmed any feelings of happiness that Ashley still had. She fell onto the couch, arms wrapped tightly around her stomach, and sobbed. The little girl in her bedroom alone was right back, on the couch now.

Her dream of "Mr. Right" meeting all her needs was extinguished like the flame of a snuffed candle. And when Ryan finally came home hours later, he and Ashley admitted they needed help.

Living the "You Must Meet Each Other's Needs" Lie

Ryan and Ashley are in trouble, and unfortunately their problems aren't unique. That's because many couples have bought into the lie that says, "I have normal, legitimate needs, some of which can only be met in marriage. When my relationship is functioning as it should, those needs are met and I feel fulfilled, whole, and complete."

As lies go, this one has been around forever. It even sneaks its way into some of the rituals we use in our Christian weddings. But the main outlets for this misleading message are popular movies and romantic songs.

Back in 1970, the group Badfinger expressed this idea in the lyrics of their hit song "Without You," which include, "I can't live, if living is without you." The lyrics aren't sophisticated, but they clearly convey a romanticized message of desperate love that became a blueprint for decades' worth of silly love songs. One line says: "I can't live, I can't give anymore."

Sounds fatal! And when you follow that sentiment back through classic literature—in Shakespeare's *Romeo and Juliet*, for example—it *was* fatal.

The classically romanticized development of love flows through three distinct and progressive stages of intensity. Love begins with simple desire: "I want you." It grows to a much fuller sentiment: "I love you." And it culminates in the all-encompassing feeling: "I need you." Obviously there must be something compelling and attractive to these ideas for them to be so enduring for so long.

Nevertheless, in spite of this idea of love's popular appeal, we've discovered that a key portion of this belief is a lie. Such thinking can even be fatal to marriage relationships when people get in the habit of telling themselves that they need their spouse to meet their needs or they will feel empty, unfulfilled, and incomplete.

Embracing the Truth About Love, Need, and Desire

Ashley's and Ryan's notions of how love develops and what are reasonable expectations in marriage violate three important truths. Let's examine each truth to see where the errors lie.

You Are Made Whole in Christ

You were individually created by the Creator of the universe, who doesn't make junk. Your faith in Christ redeems you and He completes you. You don't need another person to fill you up, and you don't need anything from your spouse in order to fully be who God created you to be.

The Bible teaches that you are a creation of God, who made you in His image (see Genesis 1:26-27). After He created the first man and woman, God took a look around, and He liked what He saw: "And God saw everything that he had made, and behold, it was very good" (Genesis 1:31). Later, sin and the Fall tarnished this created goodness, but that didn't obliterate the glory of God found in everything He made, including you and me. You are not some cosmic mistake. You're not a partial person in need of "saving" by anyone other than Christ.

The New Testament teaches that Christians have been made complete by Christ. Paul explained how this worked and warned us against believing otherwise: "See to it that no one takes you captive by philosophy and empty deceit, according to human tradition, according to the elemental spirits of the world, and not according to Christ. For in him the whole fullness of deity dwells bodily, and you have been filled in him" (Colossians 2:8-10). Paul didn't say, "Christ started you toward fullness, but now you need your spouse to finish the process." Instead, he says you have *already* been filled.

Of course, this does not mean you are perfect or sinless, or that you have everything you need or want. But it makes clear that you don't need some other person to complete you or what you were put here to accomplish.

Jesus came to make our lives complete, while our Enemy, Satan, seeks to diminish us and make us dependent on other people. "The thief comes only to steal and kill and destroy. I came that they may have life and have it abundantly" (John 10:10). Other versions translate *abundant life* as "life to the full." Don't fall for the lie that you need someone to complete you and make your life full.

Most Relational Things Cited as Needs Are Actually Desires

As humans we all have legitimate needs. Ryan and Ashley have needs. Bob and Jenni have needs. Greg and Erin have needs. However, the most basic definition of a need is something we can't live without. How many things that we commonly call needs are actually life-threatening to do without? We find it to be very few.

To survive we need food, water, and shelter, plus a few more things. To live and breathe we need God, so this is where the old song lyrics actually are true: We truly can't live without Him. Our life, our purpose, our strength, our love, and so much more are all dependent upon God.

With regard to our human relationships, though, most of what we typically call needs are really just very strong preferences. For instance, I (Bob) do need to be loved. In fact, I *am* deeply loved *by God*. This is why we are called *beloved* (which means "much loved") in 1 John 4:7. But do I need to be loved by Jenni? Truthfully, no! Now I very much want to be loved by Jenni, but whether or not she loves me has no bearing on whether I can fully be who I was created to be and do what I was created to do. Without her love I would be genuinely sad and deeply heartbroken, yet being sad and heartbroken are not life-threatening.

So why does this matter? Because in reality love is not about need—love is about desire! My love for Jenni is not because I *need* her. That sounds like dependency. My intense love for Jenni is fueled by my passionate desire. I don't *need* Jenni. I can fully be the man God created me to be either way. But I am crazy about her, and there is no one else in the world I would rather be with. She's my best friend, and she's my lover.

Interestingly, by contrast, I do need God. But even though I need Him, that's not why I love Him. My love for God is driven exercise to stay physically healthy. I need to exercise my mind to stay mentally healthy. I'm way more effective in everything when I regularly maintain my walk with God and remain spiritually healthy. And I need to tend to my heart to stay emotionally healthy.

That is what it means to be a responsible adult. Remember our diagram from chapter 2?

HEALTHY ADULT

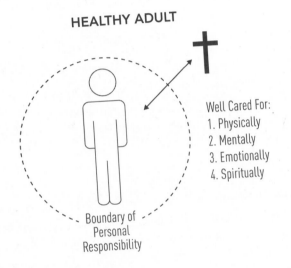

Well Cared For:
1. Physically
2. Mentally
3. Emotionally
4. Spiritually

Boundary of
Personal
Responsibility

These basics are what we believe God is calling us to daily. Remember that in John 10:10 Jesus said that the reason He came to earth was so we would have abundant life, life to the full. The great commandment then implies that from a place of fullness we give generously and sacrificially to others.

Being true to who I believe God is calling me to be, under various circumstances, might even include the sacrificial gift of giving my life. In that case, though, laying down my life for the sake of another would be an act of complete integrity. Being true to myself is caring for me.

---

by my desire to know Him and be with Him, now and forever! Then, out of an overwhelming sense of gratitude for the life He has given me, and the fate He saved me from, I am also devoted to serving Him for the rest of time.

Where this commonly causes friction and heartache in marriage is when we mistakenly think of, and present, our desires as needs. If my complaint of Jenni was "I'm not getting what I need from you, and as my wife you're the only one I can rightly get it from," and if, in fact, I was talking about a genuine need, that would be a solid argument.

However, if what I'm complaining about is actually a desire, my displeasure sounds more like a king-size temper tantrum. "I'm not getting what I want, and I really, really want it! And you need to give it to me because you have it!" I've decided I don't want to be that man anymore. That's not who my Lord created me to be. Remember, in my love story with Jenni, God writes the circumstances, Jenni writes her part, and I get to write mine.

Please note that we are not suggesting that because something is a desire rather than a need it doesn't matter, or matters less. God says to "Take delight in the LORD, and he will give you the *desires of your heart*" (Psalm 37:4, NIV, italics added). We even get into conflict over our desires (James 4:1). Apparently, He cares about our desires and He wants us to have them, just like we do. So you should know up front, our plan going forward will be to help you develop personal and relational strategies that increase the likelihood of receiving the desires of your heart, while remaining true to the person God created you to be, without compromise.

As an Adult, You Are Fully Responsible for Yourself

Couples tell us that this simple truth is probably the most empowering and transformative concept we explore with them at our intensives. But many believers struggle when we say, "You should care for yourself," because this is the opposite of everything they've been taught about the self in church and in Bible studies. To many it sounds selfish or self-centered, and aren't we supposed to "deny" ourselves and focus on the needs of others? The implication is that we should see others as better, or worth more, than us.

To add to this, many Christians unknowingly embrace a false and deadly "worm theology" that teaches human beings are worthless and making a priority to care for yourself is sinful. Worm theology has been around for centuries. The Isaac Watts hymn "Alas! And Did My Savior Bleed?" contains this wormy line: "Would he devote that sacred head for such a worm as I?" Worm theology teaches a simple message:

- We are sinners.
- Our hearts are dark.
- There is absolutely nothing good about us.

But the Bible never calls humans worms or says we are devoid of any goodness. In fact, we are so valuable that Jesus not only died for us; He assumed we were actively caring for ourselves. When someone asked Him what the greatest commandment was, Jesus' answer was clear: "You shall love the Lord your God with all your heart and with all your soul and with all your mind. This is the great and first commandment. And a second is like it: You shall love your neighbor as yourself" (Matthew 22:36-39).

However, in light of the previously discussed misunderstanding about sacrifice, many men and women we've worked with live their lives as if this verse reads: "Love your neighbor *instead of* yourself." We believe the verse says God wants us to value and care for ourselves—but in a good, godly way—first. Then we should

---

care for our neighbor with the same love and respect we show for God and ourselves.

The concept of self-care confuses many people, so let's make it perfectly clear what we're advocating.

- *Self-care is not:* Being selfish or self-centered, putting yourself first, or constantly looking out for "number one." In fact, an easy, down and dirty definition of selfishness is any time we make our own needs and desires *more* important than those of others.

- *Self-care is:* Taking full adult responsibility for yourself. It involves practicing a balanced approach toward personal health and well-being for all four aspects of a person. It differs from selfishness because you see your needs and desires not as *more* important than others' needs and desires, but just *as* important.

If you've flown on an airplane during the last thirty years, you've probably heard this kind of announcement: "If the cabin is depressurized during flight, an oxygen mask will drop down from the console above. If you are traveling with children, or if anyone around you needs help, please put *your* mask on first."

That's what self-care is all about. It's putting the oxygen mask on yourself before you attempt to help others, because if you don't do it that way, you might all die. The basic operating principle here is simply, "You can't give what you don't have." God wants us to give generously and sacrificially, but in order to give it we must first possess it.

For me, Bob, to be the best Bob I can be and have the personal resources to serve God well and give generously, I have to be fit. I need to care for the basics and get enough nutrition, rest, a exercise to stay physically healthy. I need to exercise my mind to stay mentally healthy. I'm way more effective in everything when I regularly maintain my walk with God and remain spiritually healthy. And I need to tend to my heart to stay emotionally healthy.

That is what it means to be a responsible adult. Remember our diagram from chapter 2?

HEALTHY ADULT

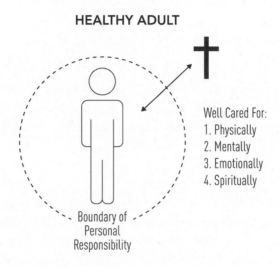

Well Cared For:
1. Physically
2. Mentally
3. Emotionally
4. Spiritually

Boundary of Personal Responsibility

These basics are what we believe God is calling us to daily. Remember that in John 10:10 Jesus said that the reason He came to earth was so we would have abundant life, life to the full. The great commandment then implies that from a place of fullness we give generously and sacrificially to others.

Being true to who I believe God is calling me to be, under various circumstances, might even include the sacrificial gift of giving my life. In that case, though, laying down my life for the sake of another would be an act of complete integrity. Being true to myself is caring for me.

care for our neighbor with the same love and respect we show for God and ourselves.

The concept of self-care confuses many people, so let's make it perfectly clear what we're advocating.

- *Self-care is not:* Being selfish or self-centered, putting yourself first, or constantly looking out for "number one." In fact, an easy, down and dirty definition of selfishness is any time we make our own needs and desires *more* important than those of others.

- *Self-care is:* Taking full adult responsibility for yourself. It involves practicing a balanced approach toward personal health and well-being for all four aspects of a person. It differs from selfishness because you see your needs and desires not as *more* important than others' needs and desires, but just *as* important.

If you've flown on an airplane during the last thirty years, you've probably heard this kind of announcement: "If the cabin is depressurized during flight, an oxygen mask will drop down from the console above. If you are traveling with children, or if anyone around you needs help, please put *your* mask on first."

That's what self-care is all about. It's putting the oxygen mask on yourself before you attempt to help others, because if you don't do it that way, you might all die. The basic operating principle here is simply, "You can't give what you don't have." God wants us to give generously and sacrificially, but in order to give it we must first possess it.

For me, Bob, to be the best Bob I can be and have the personal resources to serve God well and give generously, I have to be full. I need to care for the basics and get enough nutrition, rest, and at our intensives. But many believers struggle when we say, "You should care for yourself," because this is the opposite of everything they've been taught about the self in church and in Bible studies. To many it sounds selfish or self-centered, and aren't we supposed to "deny" ourselves and focus on the needs of others? The implication is that we should see others as better, or worth more, than us.

To add to this, many Christians unknowingly embrace a false and deadly "worm theology" that teaches human beings are worthless and making a priority to care for yourself is sinful. Worm theology has been around for centuries. The Isaac Watts hymn "Alas! And Did My Savior Bleed?" contains this wormy line: "Would he devote that sacred head for such a worm as I?" Worm theology teaches a simple message:

- We are sinners.
- Our hearts are dark.
- There is absolutely nothing good about us.

But the Bible never calls humans worms or says we are devoid of any goodness. In fact, we are so valuable that Jesus not only died for us; He assumed we were actively caring for ourselves. When someone asked Him what the greatest commandment was, Jesus' answer was clear: "You shall love the Lord your God with all your heart and with all your soul and with all your mind. This is the great and first commandment. And a second is like it: You shall love your neighbor as yourself" (Matthew 22:36-39).

However, in light of the previously discussed misunderstanding about sacrifice, many men and women we've worked with live their lives as if this verse reads: "Love your neighbor *instead of* yourself." We believe the verse says God wants us to value and care for ourselves—but in a good, godly way—first. Then we should by my desire to know Him and be with Him, now and forever! Then, out of an overwhelming sense of gratitude for the life He has given me, and the fate He saved me from, I am also devoted to serving Him for the rest of time.

Where this commonly causes friction and heartache in marriage is when we mistakenly think of, and present, our desires as needs. If my complaint of Jenni was "I'm not getting what I need from you, and as my wife you're the only one I can rightly get it from," and if, in fact, I was talking about a genuine need, that would be a solid argument.

However, if what I'm complaining about is actually a desire, my displeasure sounds more like a king-size temper tantrum. "I'm not getting what I want, and I really, really want it! And you need to give it to me because you have it!" I've decided I don't want to be that man anymore. That's not who my Lord created me to be. Remember, in my love story with Jenni, God writes the circumstances, Jenni writes her part, and I get to write mine.

Please note that we are not suggesting that because something is a desire rather than a need it doesn't matter, or matters less. God says to "Take delight in the LORD, and he will give you the *desires of your heart*" (Psalm 37:4, NIV, italics added). We even get into conflict over our desires (James 4:1). Apparently, He cares about our desires and He wants us to have them, just like we do. So you should know up front, our plan going forward will be to help you develop personal and relational strategies that increase the likelihood of receiving the desires of your heart, while remaining true to the person God created you to be, without compromise.

As an Adult, You Are Fully Responsible for Yourself

Couples tell us that this simple truth is probably the most empowering and transformative concept we explore with them

Under most normal circumstances, though, we work to stay healthy and whole while contributing generously to the lives of those around us. For us to remain optimally effective, our engines need to be firing on all cylinders.

Self-Assessment: Do I Care About Self-Care?

How well do you care for yourself? Take the quiz below to find out. You can grade yourself in these four main aspects of a well-rounded life.

Look at your grades, see which areas scored high or low, and develop a plan to practice better self-care across all four life areas where needed. The goal here is for you to be always well cared for, not to criticize yourself. God, our Dad in heaven, wants His children well cared for and blessed. In areas where you are lacking, see them as opportunities to enjoy more of the blessings you may be missing.

1. Physical: How well do I care for my body?

   a. Do I consistently eat well and follow a healthy diet?

1	2	3	4	5	6	7	8	9	10
Never				Sometimes					Always

   b. Do I regularly get enough sleep and rest?

1	2	3	4	5	6	7	8	9	10
Never				Sometimes					Always

   c. Do I engage in regular exercise and physical activity?

1	2	3	4	5	6	7	8	9	10
Never				Sometimes					Always

2. Mental: How well do I care for my mind?

a. Do I keep my mind exercised and sharp by regularly staying curious and engaged in learning new things?

1	2	3	4	5	6	7	8	9	10
Never				Sometimes				Always	

b. Do I keep my brain active by doing things like studying art, solving a crossword puzzle, reading a book, playing an instrument, memorizing Scripture, cooking, or learning a new hobby?

1	2	3	4	5	6	7	8	9	10
Never				Sometimes				Always	

c. Do I look for opportunities to regularly exchange ideas with others?

1	2	3	4	5	6	7	8	9	10
Never				Sometimes				Always	

3. Emotional: How well do I care for my heart?

a. Do I recognize and value emotions as an intentional gift from God?

1	2	3	4	5	6	7	8	9	10
Never				Sometimes				Always	

b. Am I able to accurately identify and label my own emotions?

1	2	3	4	5	6	7	8	9	10
Never				Sometimes				Always	

    c. Do I utilize my emotions, as God intended, to inform and guide my decision-making?

1	2	3	4	5	6	7	8	9	10
Never				Sometimes					Always

4. Spiritual: How well do I care for my spirit?

    a. Do I maintain an active relationship and communication with God through regular Bible study, prayer, meditation, and listening to biblical teaching?

1	2	3	4	5	6	7	8	9	10
Never				Sometimes					Always

    b. Am I led by the Holy Spirit in all decisions, seeking to fulfill my calling and purpose in life?

1	2	3	4	5	6	7	8	9	10
Never				Sometimes					Always

    c. Do I maintain regular fellowship with other Christ followers?

1	2	3	4	5	6	7	8	9	10
Never				Sometimes					Always

The Care Cycle

Emotions are a central part of our lives and a key part of God's design when He created us, but they confuse and even scare many people.

Some people seem overcome by their intense emotions, while others totally shut down their own emotional responses and blame their partner. *Ryan is the reason I feel this way, and there's really nothing I can do about it,* Ashley thinks. But none of these reactions help us much.

For instance, we completely understand why and how Ashley would blame Ryan since Ryan *did* something and Ashley *felt* something as a result; this is a basic cause and effect situation.

However, this perspective concerns us for several reasons. Most importantly, no matter what Ryan did, if Ashley's focus remains on Ryan and Ryan's behavior, Ashley remains a disempowered victim. We'd rather see Ashley well cared for and fully empowered.

But don't people do things that do cause pain and suffering in others? Absolutely yes! However, as we've unpacked these dynamics with thousands of couples, we've found it's never that simple. And if what the other person did is your main focus, your options are few and lousy.

Think about it. When Jenni would do things I (Bob) didn't like, or she hurt me, I'd usually go to her and want to talk about two things: what she did that I didn't like, and what I wanted her to do differently. In that situation, who did I see as causing the problem? Jenni, obviously. And who did I see as holding the solution? Again, Jenni. So who had all the power? Same answer. And how did she get all that power? Well, apparently, I gave it to her . . . and then I got mad because I always felt so darn powerless in our marriage!

When the Lord finally gave me the wake-up call, and I saw how I was contributing to my own misery, I shouted, "Now that's stupid! I hate feeling powerless!" I decided I was no longer going to blame Jenni for how I felt, nor look to her to make it better. I was taking the power back!

And then, when I looked deeper into the feelings I was having, I kept finding that only a portion was actually being caused by Jenni's behavior. Almost without exception there were numerous other variables—childhood experiences, insecurities I'd developed, irrational beliefs I'd acquired—that were significantly contributing to what I was feeling, and to the corresponding intensity.

That all turned out to be good news too. You see, if Jenni were causing the problem, to feel better I would normally need her to change or fix something. But Jenni has that blasted free will God gave her and, as a result, she's hard to control. Plus, even when I suceeded, I had to become a controlling person to get there—and I don't want to be that guy anymore. In either case, I can't win!

So here was the good news. To the degree I'm causing the problem, I can fix it without Jenni's cooperation or participation. Now that's empowering! I've learned to focus first and primarily on what I'm doing that's making me feel bad, and what I can do to make it better. That's not to say I ignore what Jenni does and the role she plays, but we'll address that more in later chapters. For now, I want to focus on what I have full power over.

What we're about to share with you now is a simple five-step process we've uncovered that can equip you to skillfully and successfully manage what goes on in you when you get triggered, hurt, disappointed, or angry. It's equally effective whether you're impacted by the behavior of your spouse or anyone else for that matter. This tool works no matter what your typical reaction is to your feelings. It works if you tend to get upset, it works if you easily become overwhelmed by your emotions, and it works if you're more inclined to shut down and avoid.

However, as much as I like being more empowered when Jenni and I are in conflict, we've got even better news for you. The exact same five-step process we call the Care Cycle works perfectly to help manage all aspects of caring for yourself. As you develop a little skill with this tool, all of your adult self-care responsibilities for your physical, mental, emotional, and spiritual well-being can be expertly handled too.

So let me make this perfectly clear. We're going to share one tool with five simple steps that you can use whether you are doing regular proactive self-care maintenance or whether you're upset and need help handling your reactions. This tool, when mastered, assures that you are always well cared for. It's always nice when others (like your spouse) can lend a hand, but with or without human help, you will have effective options at your disposal.

The goal is to make sure you are always well cared for, that you and all your God-given assets are valued and well managed so you remain full, whole, and healthy. It helps you to be fully who God created you to be, invest those valuable assets entrusted to your care, and fulfill all He put you here to do—no matter what any person or set of circumstances throws your way.

First, let me briefly introduce the five steps of the Care Cycle.

1. Aware

Tune into signals that alert you to your feelings. Your body sounds the first alarm: Your heart rate goes up, you start to sweat, your shoulders clench tight with tension, and a host of other indicators signal that negative emotions have kicked in. It's a little different for everybody. The key is to become conscious that you are triggered so you can make intentional choices to take good care of yourself rather than remaining in a purely reactive state. Once you "wake up" and become aware, inside it sounds something like this: *Wow, I'm triggered. Something's going on in here that needs my attention!*

2. Accept

This step can happen in a flash, but it's a two-part process. First, you need to fully accept the job of caring for yourself. You're an adult; it's your responsibility. Second, welcome your feelings, even if you don't understand them and/or they're unpleasant. Feelings are God's self-care data set. They were designed to provide the critical information about what's really going on. If you ignore or try to get rid of them, you've eliminated that data, and your ability to effectively care well for yourself is virtually gone. Instead, you'll now say to yourself something like, *Okay, this feels terrible, but my body and emotions are talking to me. I need to figure out what's going on and what I can do to make sure I stay well cared for, or I'll become useless to everyone.*

3. Allow

Even though it's your responsibility to care for yourself, God did not design you to do it alone. Prayerfully allow God to help. Note that you are not asking God to do absolutely everything for you while you simply sit there—you're asking Him for help as you care for yourself. You are still maintaining 100 percent responsibility for the job. It might sound like this: "God, I could sure use a hand here. Can you help me understand what's going on in me and what responsibly caring for myself would look like in this case? I could sure use some extra strength, wisdom, insight, and patience, because right now I'm feeling overwhelmed."

Once you've got God alongside you, if needed, you can also *allow* another person to help. He created us as communal beings, and we often function better in supportive teams. I have a number of guys I go to who can lend a hand when I'm stuck. I call them the "taking care of Bob squad." They're my support team. I can call one of them and simply say, "I'm struggling with something and could use some help sorting it out. You got a minute?"

Also, it's worth noting that nobody does more to help me than my best friend, Jenni. When appropriate, your spouse can be an incredible asset. In all cases, though, remember that as an adult you have to maintain full responsibility for the job. All support people are purely volunteers, including your spouse!

4. Attend

Now we get to work. The above steps can happen in a few seconds, but this step is where we camp out awhile to figure out what's actually going on, and what we can do to attend to it. This step involves asking lots of questions as we seek to better understand ourselves in order to devise a great self-care strategy. Ideally, the goal is to come up with options for you to do without the need of much help from anyone else, so you remain fully empowered.

Ask yourself questions like: *What am I feeling right now? What are these feelings trying to tell me? Where is this feeling coming from? Have I felt this way before? Is this feeling reminding me of something from my past? Do I believe something here that might not actually be true? What is the truth here? What am I wanting here?* Ask anything you can think of to get a clearer understanding of what's going on, where it's actually coming from, and what you want or need. Keep in mind you're working to develop a self-care plan, so more information tends to better set you up to succeed.

One quick side note: We've found that one of the most profitable questions you can ask yourself is, *Is there anything* I'm doing *that is turning up the volume and/or causing these feelings?* The more you find here, the better. If you're causing it, you can change it without any help from anyone else. That's power!

Once you have a good understanding of what's going on, shift your attention to crafting an awesome self-care plan. The best options are ones that you alone can implement. Your goal is to feel well cared for and empowered. It can include steps you can take to make yourself feel better, how to set good boundaries, how to talk to someone about a difficult or awkward situation, what you can do if the conversation doesn't go well, how to assure you keep the Lord with you in all of it, and on and on.

5. Act

Care for yourself. The best laid plans only work when they are fully implemented. Make sure that what you do internally *and* toward others is in complete integrity. That means you're acting in ways consistent with the person God designed you to be, which will also be respectful and considerate of those you are interacting with.

So those are the five steps in a nutshell, but that's not the end. We call this the Care *Cycle* because it functions as a feedback loop.

THE CARE CYCLE

Notice that when you act in caring ways toward yourself, that behavior will have an effect on you. You'll feel something as a result. Be aware of the feelings, accept them as valuable information, allow God to stay with you, and attend to them by noticing if what you did made things better. If you decide what you did is less than perfect, ask yourself if there are changes or alterations you could make to improve. Then act out those adjustments. Keep cycling around until it feels great and you feel really well cared for.

The more you do this, the more feeling well cared for becomes your norm. Over time you'll notice that many situations repeat or are similar, so you don't need to start from square one every time. You build on previous work. Practice makes perfect.

Additionally, remember that these same five steps are used to sharpen your daily proactive self-care needs. You can use this process to develop the ideal exercise regimen, determine which foods make you feel the best and which don't, which activities most powerfully feed your soul and energize you, and so on.

And maybe the best news of all is that you already do this, whether or not you realize it. We take care of ourselves continually—sometimes we do a good job; sometimes we don't. We go through a version of this process of trial and error—attending to the feedback our body, heart, mind, and spirit give—to learn what works best. Here we're just presenting it in the form of steps and a diagram, and maybe adding a few elements, so you can more easily do it on purpose. This allows you to more consciously develop this skill so you are better able to care for yourself and you know what to do when you're in trouble.

How Jenni and Bob Use the Care Cycle

Now let me show you how the five steps of the Care Cycle helped transform our marriage.

Let's say Jenni and I are having a conversation. Once again, the discussion has hit a sensitive spot in me. I'm hurt by something she said, and my body alarms have kicked in. But because I have been learning to use the Care Cycle for a while now, I'm learning how to care for myself instead of reacting in old, damaging ways.

1. Aware

As the conversation heats up, I start to sweat and my heart races. I know Jenni's words have hit a sensitive spot. (We call these sensitive spots "buttons." We'll address these in chapter 6.)

I stifle saying something sarcastic in return. I want to revert to my old ways and go full throttle at Jenni! I want to pursue an argument and follow her around the house as she tries to get away from me. Meanwhile, she would fight back or try to shut down the conflict, while I try to present my case.

I don't do that anymore. I take care of Bob. After becoming more aware of the feelings exploding inside of me and acknowledging that I'm triggered, I take my shaking self on to step two.

2. Accept

I remind myself that right now taking good care of me is *my* job. I'm no good to me, Jenni, or God if I don't. I'm not perfectly sure what I'm feeling yet, but I'm feeling strong feelings. I accept the feelings, knowing they provide me with the essential information I need to explore.

3. Allow

I go into my study and close the door. I pray and ask God to be with me. I ask Him to help me open my heart so I can hear Him and feel His love. Then I ask for His help, strength, and guidance while we figure this out. These days I spend time with God often, and I'm so grateful for His outpouring of love that self-care happens easily with Him now. I want to live there all the time.

This simple process for "allow" represents my ideal. I've noticed that getting away for a minute can really help me tune in. However, sometimes I don't have that option. When getting alone isn't available, I just pray in the moment and ask God to be with me and lend a hand in those less-than-ideal circumstances.

4. Attend

This is where I need to park, to spend the time and thought to dig into why I react about some things the way I do. The goal is for me to understand myself, and ultimately, to make sure I stay well cared for.

In this case I already know what I feel: frustrated, annoyed, and a little hurt. Actually, as I think about my responses, I feel controlled and misunderstood. Now I need to ask some questions to get a better handle on what's going on for me.

That interaction felt terrible! Why do I feel so strongly about this? Are the feelings of being controlled and misunderstood familiar to me? Argh! Yes! No wonder I reacted so strongly. This feels so much like when my mother used to try to force me to do something. There was no talking to her about it. It didn't matter how I felt or why. Just do it and do it her way! But I was different than her, and she rarely took the time to try to understand *me*. I hated that!

Am I doing anything that is either causing or amping up these feelings? In reality I'm probably reacting as if I'm ten again. Subconsciously I'm telling myself that if I let Jenni win, I'm done! I'm acting as if Jenni has power over me, and I have to fight and resist her control. As a result, oddly, it almost feels as if I'm fighting for my life. Sounds pretty melodramatic when I say it out loud; ten-year-old Bobby is back on the scene. Wow!

What is the truth here? This is Jenni, not my mother. I am a grown man, not a ten-year-old boy. I have options that weren't there before with my mom.

What do I want right now? I want to feel like a fully empowered grown man. I also want to remain true to the godly man I was created to be. I want to be kind yet firm, rather than angry and defensive.

What can I do to take good care of me, and ultimately care better for others? I'm really recognizing why I reacted so strongly. It feels good to acknowledge I'm not crazy and that the interaction with Jenni really tapped an old feeling that I've felt many times before and always hated. I think I want to tell Jenni how bad the interaction with her felt and why. Then I need to spend some time thinking about how I'd prefer to respond next time I'm in a moment like that one.

5. Act

So I let Jenni know I've given some thought to the last interaction we had and that I've realized a few things. I asked if she was in a place to hear about it. She said she was available, so I started to share.

Without blaming her at all, I let her know that my emotions were triggered by her comments, and I felt controlled and misunderstood. This became intense for me because it immediately reminded me of bad interactions I had with my mom. I said to her, "At that moment I became ten-year-old Bobby, and that's who you were talking to. I felt like I had to resist you with everything in me.

"Obviously, that was all completely unconscious. Once I realized while doing my Care Cycle what was actually going on, I reminded myself that I'm not ten and you're not my mom. If I can notice more quickly when those buttons get triggered, I don't have to react that way. I'd rather remain a grown man and be firm yet kind. I can do that!

"I also want you to know that I'm sorry I handled it like that. I know that's not the man God created me to be. I want better for me and you. Just know going forward, I'm on it."

Jenni listened and received it all with love and grace. She even shared a little about what had been going on with her during the interaction. Turned out she had a few buttons of her own getting pushed . . . but that's another story.

So after we stopped talking, I paused and tuned back in. I noticed I was having some new feelings (awareness). I accepted them, knowing they were important. I still felt God right with me. Then I asked myself, *So how did I like showing up that way, and did I end up feeling true to myself and well cared for?* In this case it was a resounding yes, in all ways. I felt well cared for and was proud of the way I handled it, with maturity, responsibility, and kindness.

Now please keep in mind, that little story represents a time I got it right the first time. I have hundreds of stories where it took a whole lot more work than that, times where I had to keep exploring and unpacking my less-than-stellar responses. I've learned a lot from both my successes and my mistakes. Together they have all contributed to me now being fairly good at caring well for myself, even under trying circumstances.

Please remember, this is a skill we're teaching here. And all skills are mastered through practice and trial and error. We don't know any other way to get there.

Self-Care Exercises

Do you want to make self-care part of your life? Here are five ways to get started.

Assess Your Self-Care

If you haven't already done so, take the Self-Care Assessment earlier in the chapter and look at your results.

Do you see any patterns?

Are there some areas where you are doing well?

Are there other areas where you fall down?

Identify priorities. Is there a poorly tended life area that requires immediate attention?

Self-care needs to be consistent and repeatable. What can you do *regularly* to care for yourself?

Share and Compare

After you and your spouse have both done your own assessments and analyzed the results, you can compare notes with each other.

Discuss any insights you saw, or decisions you made, after taking the test and weighing the results. If your spouse is open to it, discuss where you see each other's strengths and weaknesses in each of the four major self-care areas. Discuss whether you generally feel more encouraged and supported by your spouse on your self-care journey, or more discouraged and challenged. Try to stay with *sharing* information and observations rather than *criticizing* or *trying to change* your partner.

It might also be helpful for each partner to discuss ways in which their practice of self-care (or lack of practice) has been influenced by the values of our culture; the impact of their family and upbringing; and what their friends, coworkers, and other associates say and do about self-care.

Talk about Personal Responsibility

This chapter explores the lie that your spouse is supposed to meet your needs, and the truth that each partner and the marriage are best served when each practices self-care.

Discuss with your partner some of the ideas explored in this chapter: movies and song lyrics that promote the "You Must Meet Each Other's Needs" lie, thoughts about various wedding rituals you've seen and any suspect theological messages, your understanding of the need for self-care, and your reaction to the ideas on personal responsibility.

Make a Commitment You Can Keep

Fully exercising caring for self means that I take full responsibility for making sure I am well cared for mentally, physically, spiritually, and emotionally. I can't blame anyone else for the bad things I feel and think.

In the past you may not have understood self-care or practiced it as successfully as you could. Now that you're clear about that, what can you do to become more whole and healthier in all areas?

Discuss the potential ways in which exercising personal responsibility and caring for self can contribute to creating a healthier and more loving environment for you and your spouse.

Take Time for Quiet Reflection

Most people live their lives in a tumultuous state that one sociologist described as "continuous partial attention." That means they're always busy and buzzing, but never quiet, focused, and still.

If you want to learn to understand your emotions, some time alone can help. Get away for an hour or a morning, leaving behind your cell phone or other potential digital distractions. Get to know yourself. Spend some time reflecting about and exploring your own emotions.

The more you understand your own emotions and become comfortable with emotions in general, the more you and your spouse can enjoy a relationship overflowing with rich emotional sharing and satisfying intimate connection.

LOVE LIE #6:

OUR DIFFERENCES ARE IRRECONCILABLE

They had married young, at least by current standards. He was twenty-three and she was twenty-four. (That's close to the average age for first marriages sixty years ago, but ages have crept up ever since. Today the ages are twenty-nine for men's first marriages and twenty-seven for women's.)

In the beginning, everything was exciting, especially their differences.

But it didn't take long for their exciting differences to become excruciating disagreements. In fact, things blew up during their Hawaiian honeymoon when Hurricane O blew in. ("O" is their abbreviation for "Our first fight.") Their descriptions make it sound like they're talking about two separate events.

His version: It was the last day of our honeymoon. Everything had been going great, but now our time alone together was winding down and we still hadn't visited one of those beautiful Hawaiian waterfalls. After all, she had promised me that we could find a waterfall and that she would go swimming with me. Soon we would be returning to the normal world with its workaday requirements.

I was desperate for one last bit of fun. So when we arrived at a beautiful, secluded waterfall, I decided to jump into the water and experience the falls up close and personal.

"Come on in, the water's nice!" I yelled to her.

I couldn't hear her response over the roaring water, but I could tell she had declined my offer.

"Oh, honey," I shouted out, "you just ruined the honeymoon!"

Her version: It had been a good week, but I was not up for his last-day shenanigans at the waterfall. For one thing, the area was marked with big "No Swimming!" signs, which he casually ignored. I'm a nurse, and following rules is something nursing school drilled into me. A "No Swimming!" sign means just that: no swimming.

I wasn't sure why the sign was there, but I assumed there were good reasons. Perhaps swimming in this pool would disturb the breeding ground of a rare fish or an endangered salamander? Perhaps the site was dangerous, and the restriction was for people's own safety? Or perhaps the site was privately owned, and the owner didn't want anyone swimming there?

When he invited me to join him, I was not interested. Then, when he heaped blame on me about ruining the honeymoon, it was all I could take. I turned away and hiked back to the hotel for more civilized company.

Opposites Attract (and Divide)

People say that opposites attract, and they often do. That's because deep in our hearts, each one of us is aware that we have strengths and weaknesses, and we look for someone who will help balance us out and strengthen us where we are weak. Many of us figure that a marriage based on differences that complement each other will survive longer and grow stronger than a union of two similar people.

But the differences that seem so attractive when couples are dating or enjoying the first few years of marriage can turn destructive if they aren't thoroughly embraced and properly managed.

Throughout this book we're sharing stories from some of the couples we've worked with through our marriage retreats and counseling. But in this chapter, we don't need to talk about *other* couples because Greg and Erin's marriage provides a powerful example of the ways differences can attract *and* divide.

The story above about Hurricane O? That was Greg and Erin's Hawaiian honeymoon. Like many couples, they had their first real blowup during their honeymoon. Greg and Erin are not unusual in this regard, except for one thing: Greg basically assumed that having grown up in a family headed by a world-famous marriage counselor would somehow protect him from the conflicts that threaten many unions. So imagine Greg's shock when he and Erin wound up in unexpected conflicts. When they tried to work things out, things only got worse.

It seems that neither Greg nor Erin took Gary Smalley seriously enough when he warned about the dangers of unresolved conflicts and disagreements. "Every instance of conflict represents two divergent paths: you can use it to either grow together or grow apart," he wrote in *Secrets to Lasting Love*. As Gary explained:

> Conflict is inevitable in relationships. It rears its head in
> even the healthiest, most deeply intimate of marriages.
> It is how you handle conflict that will determine how it
> affects your relationship, for better or for worse. Again,
> the most important aspect is not how much you love each
> other or how committed you are to your relationship or

the strength of your faith; *optimum relationships depend on how adeptly you handle conflict.*[1]

The best marriage researchers say they can predict with a high degree of certainty if a marriage will succeed or fail based on how a couple deals with conflict. If they argue without ever resolving their issues or consistently avoid conflict altogether, their marriage is at risk for divorce.

That's because poorly managed conflict doesn't go away. Unresolved issues are merely buried alive, where they often fester until they become much bigger problems. In the long run, unresolved conflicts can end up exploding like a massive volcano, leaving both you and your spouse in the wake of destruction.

Falling for the Lie

Greg probably should have known better. No marriage is immune. Conflict is unavoidable. The apostle Paul warned that married couples *will* face many troubles in this life (1 Corinthians 7:28). But his disappointment was making him fall for Love Lie #6—one of the most popular love lies there is—the belief that significant differences inevitably drive people apart.

You may believe that conflict necessarily divides if you grew up in a combustible home where your parents fought all the time and never really resolved issues. The same might be true if your parents never fought but instead just "got along," which means they tried to avoid conflict altogether. When two people don't talk about the conflicts big and small that happen in everyday life, they coexist like two ships silently passing in the night, or simply live together as "roommates" rather than as friends and lovers.

Maybe you or someone you know has heard the words *irreconcilable differences* in divorce court. This may be the most commonly cited reason for divorce today. The obvious idea here is that, in the end, a couple's differences are what make the marriage unworkable. They may not have initially viewed those differences as a problem—they may have even enjoyed them. But as time moves on, and their differences bump into competing desires and expectations, it's like the differences are magnified and seem to become insurmountable.

We continually hear statements like:

"We're just too different."

"We want completely different things in life."

"We have nothing in common."

"We're headed in two totally different directions."

Turning the Inevitable into the Beneficial

It's true that differences can and often do lead to conflict. But we're convinced that the differences are not the problem. Differences were created by God on purpose, with purpose. They are meant to be the blessing that makes you better as a couple. Male and female he created them (Genesis 5:2). The problems come from not knowing how to identify the value of those differences and how to adequately utilize them for the benefit of the team.

We even go so far as saying that differences are *never* the true underlying problem in a marriage. You may find that hard to believe, but we spend a lot of time unraveling marital messes. The problem is how we handle the conflicts that naturally arise every time we're in relationship with another human being, who by design is different from us. And the unfortunate result is that the conflicted couple has lost the ability to take advantage of what God meant to be a blessing.

What is it that enables some couples to thrive amid significant personality differences while other couples continually squabble over each and every perceived slight? Pastor and author Max

Lucado points to the answer: "Conflict is inevitable, but combat is optional."[2]

Not only is combat optional—we have even better news for you: If you and your spouse can learn how to handle conflict in healthy ways, you will experience greater trust, openness, mutual respect, and other bonds that help love and intimacy grow.

It's amazing but true: If we learn how to handle the natural conflicts that typically arise between us as we live our lives, conflict can actually be our pathway to deeper intimacy as we learn to take full advantage of our differences. We learn to make those differences work for us rather than against us!

We now want to share some ideas of how you can take full advantage of the amazing opportunity you have as a result of being married to someone really different from you, and what to do when the inevitable conflicts do arise. Toward that end we want to make sure you understand a basic tenet we subscribe to.

We totally reject the idea that the ends justify the means. Many people either believe, or act as if they believe, that it doesn't matter how you get there, as long as you end up in a good place. It's hard for us to calculate how much damage and pain has resulted from marital battles, regardless of whether they got to a resolution or not.

Therefore we believe that how you get from point A to point B is every bit as important as where you end up. We're proposing that couples approach working through differences and dealing with conflict only using methods that are respectful and kind, as if you're actually dealing with someone you like (maybe even love!) rather than an enemy. We're suggesting that, in the long run, you can't afford to have marital conflict lead to casualties.

We're not even going to teach you "fair fighting" rules. I fight with an adversary. My spouse is *never* my enemy! My spouse is my friend and my lover. I (Bob) wish I had recognized that sooner. In my conflicts with Jenni, I frequently acted as if I had a "may the best man win" mentality. My regret over the pain we've both experienced is ongoing. Our home now is a no-fight zone. We still deal with conflicts and differences but handle them with tremendous respect and care—as friends would.

Greg and Erin have done much work to address conflict in their own marriage and in their work with other couples. So Greg will take over the chapter as he willingly dissects his own marriage for your edification. Bob will be back at the end.

Our Differences Needn't Divide Us

My theory is simple. The younger people are when they get married, the more likely they are to marry someone dramatically different from them. That was clearly the case with Erin and me.

When you're younger, you're sometimes painfully aware of your personal deficits and the many holes in your life. We often try to fill those holes with other people. That was what happened when I met Erin. I was twenty-three and there was a lot missing in me. By comparison, the things I saw in Erin were so different and so wonderful. Exotic even! She complemented me so well in so many ways. I felt like she filled in many of the holes in me.

Then Hurricane O rolled in and revealed that marriage is much more complicated than I realized. The gaps between us needed something stronger than crack filler. As we learned early on, personality differences are real and can't be ignored or dismissed. They must be navigated and hopefully utilized to our benefit.

I had always loved Erin's outgoing personality, but we were still early in our marriage when I realized I had a problem. She wanted to have people over to our little apartment every single night. While I enjoyed many of these friends and the fun evenings we had together, the never-ending series of social evenings was becoming too much for me.

I tried to talk to Erin about it, but the conversation started out somewhat one-sided.

Greg: "Honey, all these people are wearing me out! It seems like we always have people over. Don't you ever want to spend any time alone with me?"

Erin: (Silence, followed by more silence, punctuated by curious looks and a rapid blinking of the eyes.) "What do you mean, dear?"

Now it was my turn to say something. But what? Can you see the conflict brewing? I knew from past experience that the conversation could go in a variety of directions, many of them potentially destructive. We'll show you the best method we've found for resolving disagreements in chapter 9. But first we want to talk about *why* these conversations turn into conflict.

When Conversations Go South

How do you respond when a conflict appears on your radar? Do you run and hide? Do you grab it by the throat and try to wrestle it into submission? People respond to conflict in differing ways, which means that some couples find themselves in conflict about how to handle conflict!

However, what we now know is that there's an insidious pattern to conflict that our true Enemy, Satan, understands and utilizes to his benefit and our detriment. Surprisingly, we've discovered that this same pattern occurs beneath all marital struggles. Most of us are completely unconscious of the pattern and therefore are at its mercy. Satan, however, is more than aware of it and plays it fully to his advantage.

Our best defense against this sinister pattern of destruction is *awareness.* Once we clearly see what is going on, we're able to take evasive action. We are no longer available to be played like puppets. We become empowered to stop the futile madness and set out on a course toward success and victory.

We want to break down the cycle of futility and its various components piece by piece so you can become fully aware of what's happening, what contributes to it, and how to single-handedly stop it. We'll start by continuing to highlight our God-given differences.

Our Journey down the Rabbit Hole

Erin is more adventurous. I'm more cautious.

Erin is more impulsive. I like to plan ahead.

Erin likes for the two of us to hop in our car and just start driving—destination to be determined. I like to map things out.

These are the facts of our relationship. There's no denying that when God created the two of us, variety and diversity were foremost in His mind.

To look at just one of these examples in detail: Precisely how much do I like to map things out? When I travel for meetings or to speak, I play it by the book:

- I always fly United. I know their routes, their ticketing and reservation system, and their baggage rules. Plus I fly so much with them that I get to hang out in their airport clubs—a real relief after a rough trip.

- I always rent from Hertz. I realize the auto rental industry is very competitive, but I know how to find the Hertz shuttles, which lines to stand in, and where I go to choose my car.

- I always stay at Hilton hotel properties. I know how they work, and I feel comfortable there.

(Note: None of these companies has reimbursed me for these unsolicited endorsements, but advertising directors seeking a new spokesman for their TV commercials should call my agent!)

Erin thinks my travel routines sound incredibly boring. They are, and that's precisely why I follow them so rigorously. Travel-related details overwhelm me, so I compensate through routine.

Most of the time Erin and I are good with our differences, but even the smallest discussions can turn divisive when we forget how different we are. That was certainly the case the evening I got home from a long day at work and Erin suggested we go out to eat at a restaurant in downtown Colorado Springs called The Rabbit Hole.

Erin was cranked up and excited. I was worn out and suspicious.

Erin was ready for an open-ended adventure. I wanted to map things out.

Not only do I like my journeys by air travel done by the book; that's the way I prefer to do it when driving around town too. Erin pictured a fun drive followed by a delectable meal at an exciting new restaurant; I pictured a drive on a crowded interstate, a few wrong turns onto one-way streets in the center of town, and being forced to park miles from the restaurant.

Erin and I have learned (by trial and error) how to manage our differences. The key is to value that we are different. Instead of seeing Erin's spontaneous and adventurous personality as bothersome, I now see that as a valuable gift in our marriage. If it weren't for Erin's daring personality, I'd be a lonely recluse. But Erin also values how I like to plan to be spontaneous. I know that sounds like an oxymoron—*plan* and *spontaneous* are contradictory words. Because we value our differences, we've learned how to meld them into a workable solution. How this works for us is that Erin will suggest a new restaurant like The Rabbit Hole, and then I'll quickly research the best route and parking via my smartphone. Erin gets the thrill of going on a new adventure, and I get the security of knowing where I'm going and the best parking spot. This is a true win-win solution for managing our differences.

We are really different by design. So are you. As a starting point to understand the natural cycle of conflict, let's take a quiz to identify any basic differences in personality between you and your partner.

What's Your Personality Profile?

God creates each one of us as unique persons. There are no carbon copies when it comes to humans. This human diversity is what makes marriage frustrating at times, but our differences also make marriage exciting and life-changing.

My father, Gary Smalley, and John Trent created a personality profile quiz that couples can use to discover what makes each one of them tick. Some couples have more dramatically different personalities than others; some are more similar. However, unless you feel like you're staring in the mirror when you look at your spouse, you *are* different! Appreciating those differences, and allowing them room, is the beginning of embracing God's magnificent plan for your marriage.

Please go to www.focusonthefamily.com/marriage/4-animals -personality-test to take the personality profile quiz, and take it right now. Ideally, you and your partner can each take the quiz and compare notes. Use the quiz to better understand your partner's God-given differences and to see how the two of you possess strengths and weaknesses in different areas.

Pushing Each Other's Buttons

With our God-given differences now in focus, let's start unveiling the destructive cycle of conflict that our Enemy uses to take us down. The more clearly we see it, the less likely we are to unconsciously spin in it and the less power Satan, and our cycle of conflict, will have over us.

Have you ever noticed when you and your spouse argue that

the fight often has an eerily memorable flavor no matter what you are disagreeing about? Do you think, *This feels strangely familiar, like we've been here before*? It's almost like a recurring dream (or nightmare!). The typical issues most people disagree about include:

- Money
- Household chores
- Children
- Sex

- Work
- Leisure time
- In-laws

These are the topics you *think* are driving the conflict, but often they're not. That's an illusion. We do understand that there are real underlying issues in marriage that need resolution, and we will address how to manage those effectively and successfully as we continue. However, we've also discovered that the "juice" that commonly charges up those interactions is more than meets the eye.

Here's what's *really* happening during arguments that go south: One of your "buttons" got pushed.

Buttons? We've all got them. They're your tender spots. The places where you are most vulnerable. The sensitive places in your heart that are easily triggered, usually because they reflect something unpleasant or painful from your past. They may be there because of a single incident or because of repeated, related circumstances over the years.

There are no ways to avoid having these buttons. We live in a fallen world, with imperfect, fallen people. There is no way we know of to walk through this life without getting stung along the way. No matter how wonderful your family and childhood were, pain, fear, and sadness touch us all.

Buttons often take us to deep, sometimes dark emotions that

evoke mysterious feelings or patterns of thought inside us that frequently remain outside of our normal awareness. We may not immediately be able to pinpoint exactly which button got pushed, but we sure feel that one did.

Have you ever been in a conversation where buttons are being pushed? One moment you're having a conversation with your spouse about money or household chores, and the next minute one or both of you suddenly feel:

- unloved
- disrespected
- rejected
- like a failure
- controlled
- abandoned

- inadequate
- worthless
- not good enough
- invalidated
- unimportant
- misunderstood

It's easy to tell when buttons get pushed in a conversation with your partner. Typically, the feelings escalate quickly and become intense. A conversation that begins with questions such as "Well, where do you think we can trim our budget?" leads to you feeling like this: *You don't really love me. No one ever really loved me!*

Now that may be a bit of an exaggeration, but sometimes not by much.

Buttons Galore

Our buttons can be triggered by specific words, events, or circumstances. We never see it coming, but once a button is pushed, we experience a strong emotional charge. Old memories emerge. Complex feelings flood over you. You momentarily lose control of your behavior.

Some people become extremely emotional. There's no reason and rationality when you respond to a button. It's off to the races with pure, powerful emotions. At first, this generally happens below our conscious awareness.

Have you ever had a conversation where afterward you stop and say, "Why in the world did I ever say *that* horrible thing to the person I love?" Your button was pushed. Maybe more than one.

Have you ever slammed a door? Cursed under your breath? Thrown a plate? Kicked the dog? Your button was pushed.

As we've said, this happens to us all. It happens quickly and below our conscious awareness. However, just because it begins in the unconscious realm doesn't mean it has to stay there. But it's almost impossible to avoid.

Greg and Erin's Guide to Button Pushing

Pushing another person's buttons is incredibly easy. Erin and I know, because we did it all the time. Here's how one of our real-world conversations played out:

Greg has just come in from the garage after driving home from a long day at work. He sees Erin is busy and offers to help.

"Honey, it looks like you have a lot going on. Is there anything I can help you with?"

Erin has been going nonstop all day and is now corralling rambunctious kids, cooking a nice dinner, and loading the dishwasher. She hears Greg speak to her, but the main word she hears is *you*.

Somewhere deep within, a button or two are pushed. This is how her feelings translate what he is saying: *Housework is your work. I have more important things to do.*

So this is how Erin reacts to Greg: "Thanks, but I know you have important things to do, so I can take care of all this."

Greg is shocked. Dumbfounded. Lots of button activity! He had reached out to Erin in love, with an offer of help. But how did she respond? Frankly, it felt like she had overreacted.

So this is how Greg reacts to Erin: "Relax! I was just trying to help. You don't have to bite my head off!"

Ladies and gentlemen, they're off to the races! As you can probably imagine, this interaction set in motion a relational spin that can quickly look like a merry-go-round.

So What's Really Happening Here?

When our buttons get pushed, we feel something, and generally we don't like the feeling. So we do something to try to make the feeling go away. That's our reaction, and it's almost always a knee-jerk response. Rarely do we give it much thought. We react! It looks something like this:

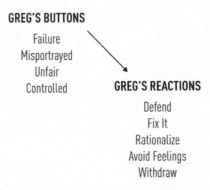

GREG'S BUTTONS

Failure
Misportrayed
Unfair
Controlled   **GREG'S REACTIONS**

Defend
Fix It
Rationalize
Avoid Feelings
Withdraw

Greg's buttons are tender spots that feel like bruises. Some of his biggest are feeling like a failure, feeling misportrayed, feeling that things are unfair, and feeling controlled.

What happens when one or more of his buttons are pushed?

His heart closes (remember the roly-poly bugs in chapter 3?), and he reacts. People typically react with one of three reactions:

- Fight (engaging in argument)
- Flight (fleeing from conflict)
- Freeze (paralyzed by fear)

In Greg's case, when any of those buttons are pushed, his natural knee-jerk reaction will be to defend himself, try to fix it, rationalize, seek to avoid his feelings, and/or withdraw. All of the reactions are an attempt to make the unpleasant feelings go away.

Likewise, Erin has her own buttons. She doesn't like those feelings either.

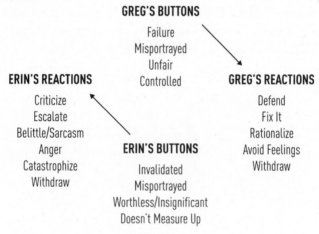

GREG'S BUTTONS
Failure
Misportrayed
Unfair
Controlled

ERIN'S REACTIONS
Criticize
Escalate
Belittle/Sarcasm
Anger
Catastrophize
Withdraw

GREG'S REACTIONS
Defend
Fix It
Rationalize
Avoid Feelings
Withdraw

ERIN'S BUTTONS
Invalidated
Misportrayed
Worthless/Insignificant
Doesn't Measure Up

Like Greg, and all the rest of us, when any of her buttons get pushed, Erin will typically react in one of her rehearsed ways, quickly and without much thought. She, too, wants those feelings gone.

Over the years, what we've found happens next is both bizarre and predictable. No matter who first has a button pushed and reacts, if they are anywhere near their spouse, it will almost always push the button of the other. We call it the Reactive Cycle, and it looks like this:

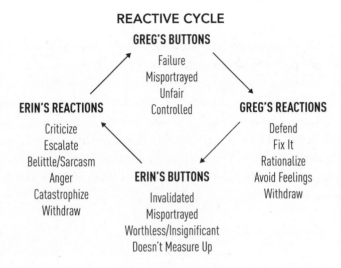

REACTIVE CYCLE

GREG'S BUTTONS
Failure
Misportrayed
Unfair
Controlled

ERIN'S REACTIONS
Criticize
Escalate
Belittle/Sarcasm
Anger
Catastrophize
Withdraw

GREG'S REACTIONS
Defend
Fix It
Rationalize
Avoid Feelings
Withdraw

ERIN'S BUTTONS
Invalidated
Misportrayed
Worthless/Insignificant
Doesn't Measure Up

This cycle of button, reaction, button, reaction can amp up quickly and intensely. Remember the merry-go-round? We all hate how it feels.

So what do people normally do to stop the madness? When Greg's buttons are pushed, where will he naturally focus his energy and attention?

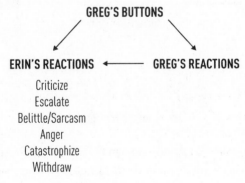

GREG'S BUTTONS

ERIN'S REACTIONS ◀——— GREG'S REACTIONS
Criticize
Escalate
Belittle/Sarcasm
Anger
Catastrophize
Withdraw

He'll try to get Erin to stop or change her reactions. It makes sense, but that strategy immediately hurts everyone. How much righteous power and control does Greg have over Erin's free will? None! In order to get Erin to change her behavior, he has to figure out how to convince her to act differently. As a result, she will normally feel invalidated, judged, criticized, and unloved.

And to make matters worse, if Greg succeeds in manipulating and/or controlling her into behaving differently (even if it's better for her in the end), he's had to become manipulative and controlling to get there. It's not how the Lord handles us when we use our will poorly. We know Greg ultimately wants to be more conformed to the image of our Lord. So it's both not the man Greg wants to be, and it's not the man God has called him to be.

Stopping the Madness

So what can we righteously and effectively do to break the cycle? Where does our responsibility and power actually lie?

Remember, as a fully functioning adult, Greg is responsible for Greg. How he shows up, regardless of what comes at him, is ultimately what he will be responsible for when he stands before God. So in the Reactive Cycle, Greg is responsible for how he feels (his buttons) and what he does (his reactions).

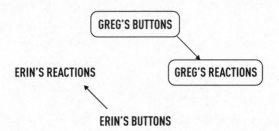

The good news is this is also where his power lies. We've found that it only takes one person to stop the reactive spin, and either

Greg or Erin can do it without the cooperation of the other. Now that's power!

So what can Greg do? Create *space*.

$$\text{GREG'S BUTTONS} \xrightarrow[\text{SPACE}]{\text{CREATE}} \text{GREG'S REACTIONS}$$

$$\text{ERIN'S REACTIONS} \longleftarrow \text{ERIN'S BUTTONS}$$

Typically, when we encourage people to create space and then ask them what we mean, they think we're talking about space between them and their spouse. While we recognize that sometimes that is helpful, that's not what we mean here. We're talking about creating space between your buttons and your reaction. That's what breaks the cycle. That's where your power lies.

You see, the Reactive Cycle can only continue if both people are involved in it, much like a tug-of-war. If two people are holding the rope, pulling in opposite directions, and either drops the rope, that game is over. In the Reactive Cycle, if either of you does not react, the cycle ends. Erin can't continue with Greg if Greg won't play. She may stay upset, but the cycle between them ends.

Now, realistically, not reacting can feel like it requires superhuman strength! It demands a powerful level of self-control. In fact, when Greg is able to muster the self-control needed to not react, he may walk away flexing his muscles, saying to himself, *You stud. Any normal man would have reacted to his wife when she said that, but you resisted. Way to go!*

And Erin is just as capable of exercising that much self-control and power to stop the madness. Both benefit when either stops the cycle. The Reactive Cycle is a go-nowhere spin for all parties involved.

As you create some space between your buttons and your reactions, let your partner know you're not walking away. You're taking a time-out to get your heart back open, and you'll try to finish the discussion as soon as you can.

Taking a time-out is not the same as withdrawing. Withdrawing from interaction is an extremely deadly "flight" reaction. Long-term withdrawal leads to emotional distance. But calling a time-out is a coping strategy designed to prepare you to reengage in the conversation.

Marriage research indicates that you might need about twenty minutes to calm down when your buttons have been pushed. Our rule is that the person who calls the time-out should be the person who reconvenes the conversation.

Buttons are real, and we can't tell when they will be pushed. The Reactive Cycle is real too. Once people's buttons are pushed, they typically cycle through the potentially harmful emotional reactions that can destroy marriages. And even though you can't erase or do away with your buttons, you can deal with them in a healthy way by discerning when they are pushed and learning to keep them from raining down anger and insults on the person you love and the relationship you care so much about.

Do What Instead?

Certainly, stopping the cycle is better than continuing. But many people get concerned because it sounds like we're encouraging their already-avoidant spouse to withdraw further—and praising them for it.

Fortunately, nothing could be further from the truth. Clearly, it's better to not stay engaged in a Reactive Cycle because everybody gets hurt there. But while just creating space does stop the madness, it doesn't take you to any better place personally or relationally.

What you do in the space is what determines whether it moves things forward to a better place.

Let's return for a moment to our diagram of a healthy marriage.

HEALTHY MARRIAGE MODEL

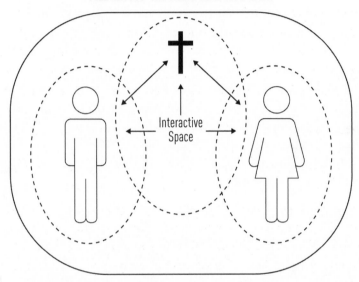

The Reactive Cycle occurs in the Interactive Space and results in an ineffective and unpleasant interaction between husband and wife. When either breaks that cycle, they interrupt the interaction and temporarily step out of the inner circle. Because both their responsibility and power lie in their personal circles, that's where their attention must go.

Generally, the person who breaks the cycle is having strong, unenjoyable feelings (buttons pushed) and is tempted to close her or his heart and react in unfortunate, un-Christlike ways. But this spouse resisted and now has the opportunity to reconnect with God, open up his or her heart, and care well for himself or herself before doing or saying anything else. This is where the Care Cycle, outlined in the previous chapter, becomes useful. And once this person feels reopened and well cared for and is reconnected to God, he or she can step back into the inner circle and reengage his or her spouse in a respectful and loving manner.

We realize we haven't yet given you clear, solid tools and instruction in how to reengage safely and effectively, but we're almost there!

In the following three chapters, we will be sharing three important principles and tools. First, we'll share how to create the ideal safe and secure marital environment to most easily enable your marriage to thrive. Second, we'll show you how to safely and effectively talk about emotionally charged topics to assure that both of you feel understood and cared for. And third, we'll describe how to deal with differences and resolve conflict so that you always end with a win-win outcome.

Making Conflict Work for You

No matter how your parents handled (or didn't handle) conflict, you can create a new legacy for *your* marriage and family. You have the opportunity to use conflict—those times when you're hurt, annoyed, frustrated, wounded, confused, angry, and discouraged with one another—to actually grow closer together.

We're not giving you fancy double-talk or a sales pitch. This is how we live out our marriages, and this is how we help couples handle the inevitable conflicts that will occur in their relationships simply because they are different.

Sadly, many couples don't see the potential value of conflict because of past negative experiences. Maybe they didn't see healthy conflict modeled growing up, or they haven't handled disagreements successfully over the course of their marriage. But when you and your partner learn to manage your conflicts in a healthy way, both of you will actually feel safer. You will be more willing to open your hearts and reveal who you really are. You will create a marriage where being two different people is not only tolerated; it is prized. This is true intimacy.

Conflict can be a doorway to this kind of intimacy, as our good friend and relationship guru Dr. Gary J. Oliver put it: "Conflict is the process we go through and the price we pay for intimacy. Intimacy is always achieved at the price of facing our differences and negative feelings, listening, understanding and resolving them."[3]

As you make conflict work for you, both of you will experience more of the love and healing you never fully experienced when your buttons and reactions were ruling the day. Couples who learn the lesson of conflict management will find conflict helps them in many ways. It can:

- bring problems into the light
- provide an opportunity to break old, ineffective patterns
- help you to better appreciate the differences between you and your spouse
- give you a chance to care for and empathize with your spouse
- humble you (James 4:6 says that God "gives grace to the humble")
- give you great insight into your own personal issues— especially the ones you bring with you into marriage. We all have them, and they repeatedly show up in our views, our reactions, and our perspectives of our spouse and situations.
- cause you to grow into a healthier individual and ultimately a healthier husband or wife
- help you learn how to anticipate and resolve future conflicts

- bring you closer together as you listen, understand, and validate each other
- raise you to higher levels of marital satisfaction every time you manage the conflict well
- be the sole reason for the amazing experience of "make-up sex"[4]

Exercises for Managing Your Buttons and Reactive Cycle

Don't React

The key to breaking the Reactive Cycle is to create space between your button and your reaction—this means *don't react*! It takes self-control to stop the cycle, and if you are really triggered, it may feel like it takes superhuman strength, but you can do it! Developing this level of self-control can feel like one of the single most empowering things you can do. The cycle can only continue if both people are participating, so you can single-handedly stop the cycle by choosing not to react. You may need to take a deep breath and step back. As soon as possible, enter into the Care Cycle, care well for yourself, and figure out what is going on for you so you can get and keep your heart open and remain true to the person God created you to be.

Call a Time-Out

If you leave without letting your spouse know what you're doing, it feels like withdrawal, and he or she will probably follow you around the house. I (Greg) say something like this to Erin: "I love you and want to hear you, but right now I'm pretty shut down, and I'm unable to really listen to you. I'm taking a quick time-out, but I'll be back to finish our discussion." Notice that I'm not asking Erin's permission. Instead, I'm letting her know that I need a break, but I'll be back. We've made a rule that whoever calls a time-out has to initiate getting us back together to finish our conversation. The difference is that our hearts will be open, and we'll be better able to really listen.

What about you? Talk to your spouse about what you can say in the moment that that will help him or her to understand that you are taking a time-out and aren't withdrawing. Maybe it's a special phrase such as "Code Red" or a signal (for example, the time-out signal that basketball players make). It could be a funny word like *platypus*. Whatever you come up with, make sure that the meaning is that you're taking a break but will return.

Accept Your Feelings and Move On

The powerful feelings both you and your spouse experience should not be judged as good or bad, right or wrong. Rather, they should be seen as providing you with valuable information you need. When powerful feelings arise, treat them with curiosity for the purpose of providing valuable information about you and your spouse. Take a few minutes to discuss each other's buttons and reactions. Remember that your goal is not to judge or fix but simply to understand and care.

Study Your Reactions

Have you ever been surprised by how you can react when your buttons are pushed? We want you to study those reactions. Reactions don't happen by accident. Your reactions are intended to get a certain result. In essence, reactions operate as strategies, even if they are largely unconscious strategies. What result are you trying to achieve through each reaction? What underlying desires motivate you to use that strategy as a way to get your "want"?

How did you come up with your ideas about how to handle conflict? Was it from watching your parents, seeing someone else do it, or just a creative moment of inspiration? How consistently or successfully do your reactions get the desired results?

Map Your Reactive Cycle

We showed how a conversation between Greg and Erin spun out of control as each one pushed the other's buttons.

Take a close look at how both of you react. Write down some examples of your Reactive Cycles when different buttons are pushed. Map this out and share it with your spouse. Then consider and discuss possible ways you each can demonstrate caring toward the other when your buttons have been pushed.

LOVE LIE #7:

I'M GONNA MAKE YOU LOVE ME

Education first.
  Career second.
  Marriage and family third.
  Becky and Randy grew up hundreds of miles from each other in families that couldn't be more different, but both of them received the exact same message from their parents: Instead of falling in love and getting married in their teens or early twenties, they should focus first on studying hard and working hard so they could establish themselves financially. Then, and only then, should they give in to love and its many joys and obligations.

The message hit home, and both of them basically did as instructed. In spite of each quietly longing for the day they found that special someone, they completed undergraduate and graduate degrees in their fields and landed high-paying jobs that set them on the road to stable, lucrative careers.

Now, it was time to finally get serious about romance and relationships. The two of them found each other at a Houston-area social gathering for upwardly mobile thirtysomething single professionals.

Becky worked as an anesthesiologist at a local hospital while Randy was an engineering manager for an international firm. Both owned pricey condos, nice cars, and closets full of athletic gear that remained largely unused because of their busy schedules. They traded business cards and said they would be in touch soon. Becky didn't expect much to happen, so she was surprised when Randy called her two days later and invited her to dinner. She graciously accepted, but it would be two weeks before they could both find an open evening for their first date.

When they finally got together, they had a great evening. They enjoyed each other and had much in common. In addition to the work ethic they had inherited from their parents, both were committed to Christ, though neither had yet had much success in finding a church they liked. They decided that first night that they would start seeing each other during the week. In time they added a regular weekend commitment, visiting churches they thought might be a fit.

They both fell in love with a five-hundred-member nondenominational church they visited, and that's where they were married after nearly three years of dating. She was thirty-three and he was thirty-six.

Now, after years of putting education first, career second, and relationships third, Becky and Randy are finally ready to make love a priority.

Is This All There Is?

Over the next three years, they welcomed a son and daughter into their big new house. Life was good, and busy with work and kids, but Randy and Becky shared a commitment to their individual spiritual growth. She joined a women's Bible study that met on

Saturdays at the church, and he became part of a men's group that met for early breakfasts every Wednesday. Their career gains continued, with Randy getting a big promotion at his engineering firm. The kids were healthy and happy. Randy and Becky also continued to enjoy a decent sexual relationship.

But both of them noticed something curious as they got to know the members of their small groups. Three of the women in Becky's group said they were happily married and often shared details about their relationships. But the three others were quieter when the topic of marriage came up, confiding to the group that they were dissatisfied with the lack of real closeness in their relationships.

"It's like we're two ships passing in the night," said one of the women, who claimed she felt "stuck" in her relationship with her husband.

Driving home from her Bible study one Saturday, Becky replayed in her mind the things the women in her group had said. Their marriages seemed to fit into one of two camps. There were those who enjoyed meaningful relationships with their husbands, spending time alone together, engaging in deep conversations about their thoughts and feelings, and sharing close spiritual connections with God and each other.

Then there were those who described their relationships with their husbands like roommates or business partners. By the time she had arrived back home, Becky had become increasingly convinced that she and her husband lived like the people in the second group. She had known it for a while but had been hiding her true feelings—both from her husband and from herself.

Randy noticed a similar scenario in his group. While two of the men would joke about their healthy sexual relationships with their wives, the other three men were more reticent, with one admitting he and his wife had not had sex in many months.

"I feel like Jane and I are coadministrators of a family business," said one of the men, "not friends or lovers." That comment struck Randy, who had long felt that his relationship with Becky had become less of a romance and more of a business relationship focused on managing the kids, the household, and their careers.

By the time Becky and Randy celebrated their fifth wedding anniversary, their passion seemed to be cooling while the pressures of work and family continued to heat up. The two of them expressed their frustrations in different ways, but there was a similar theme in their complaints.

"I looked forward to this relationship for all my life," Becky said to the women in her group. "Now I'm wondering if *this* is all there is?"

Meanwhile, Randy now had something in common with a couple of the other men in his group. "We've become so disconnected we're hardly even having sex anymore!" he confessed to the men one Wednesday morning. Becky had begun rejecting his overtures two weeks ago.

Both Randy and Becky had waited years for the fulfillment marriage promised, and while they were grateful for the companionship and were generally pleased with the relationship, something was missing. Both now wanted more: something deeper and more meaningful and satisfying.

"I have business meetings with people all the time," said Randy, who had noticed his marriage becoming more functional than flourishing. "I don't want that kind of relationship at home."

Becky felt the same way. "I have meaningful conversations all day with my coworkers and patients," she told the women in her group. "But at home? Not so much."

We met Becky and Randy at one of our intensives, where we've met many couples over the years who are struggling to experience more closeness and connection in their marriages. These couples use similar language to express their frustrations to us, saying they feel more like business partners, roommates, friends, cohabitants, or even "friends without benefits" rather than loving husbands and wives.

Many couples don't talk much about these issues between themselves, although most have tried. Some fear that honestly sharing their feelings will only make matters worse, or even risk the survival of the relationship. Better to remain quiet and hope for the best, we hear them say.

"If I remain superficially peaceful, things are calm," said one of the women in Becky's group. "But if I rock the boat by speaking up about the deep, unmet longings in my heart, things will only become painful."

Designed for Intimacy

As stated early in this book and reiterated throughout, we believe that human beings are created for intimacy. When God made each one of us, He designed us for close, caring relationships. Pretty much every one of us hungers to be truly close and connected to others, but not every one of us experiences this kind of deep connection with another person. Some men and women say they desire this type of intimacy—even though they may not be willing to risk the emotional vulnerability required to make it happen. Others admit they really don't know what it is they're searching for.

In chapter 2 we offered a simple definition: At its core, true intimacy is the journey of really getting to know someone over time. Biblically it's the idea of "knowing and being known."

- *Knowing* means taking the time and being present to engage in the hard work required to understand your partner from the inside out.

- *Being known* means being open, honest, vulnerable, and giving another person the keys to unlock your heart of hearts, which means allowing your spouse to truly know you.

This kind of connection isn't something that always happens between two people, at least not immediately. It takes time to develop. And in its more meaningful and satisfying forms, it doesn't happen by accident or on its own. A relationship developing depth occurs best when two people intentionally make getting to know each other an ongoing priority. Scripture gives us a picture of this process in describing the growth of our love for God: "For now we see in a mirror dimly, but then face to face. Now I know in part; then I shall know fully, even as I have been fully known" (1 Corinthians 13:12).

Your relationship to your spouse should mirror your relationship to your Creator: growing in honesty and vulnerability over time. Marriage counselors debate whether two human beings can ever be fully known to each other, but we've seen couples who get pretty close to this kind of relationship transparency. However, in the end success is less about *fully* knowing your spouse than *desiring* to know them better, while *pursuing* getting to know them. As a result, while you learn and grow through life and share those experiences with each other, your friendship grows and your closeness and connection deepens.

As we've seen, Becky's and Randy's individual experiences in their relationship and their talks with their small groups have them worried about the level of real closeness in their own marriage. "Some couples never seem to really connect, or they somehow lost it," Randy said. And he's right.

This quest for greater closeness and connection explains why a seemingly endless number of relationship "experts" offer advice online for those seeking a deeper type of bonding with their partners. Google the words *increase intimacy* and you'll see what we mean.

Randy found an article on one website that warmed his engineer's heart: "Three Scientifically Proven Ways to Increase Intimacy." Becky found a different article online that appealed to her feeling of being overworked and overbooked: "Eight Ways to Increase Intimacy in 5 Minutes or Less."

We're all for emotional intimacy, and as you'll soon see, we have some unique ideas about how to cultivate this kind of closeness. But we worry when online "experts," authors, or counselors embrace Love Lie #7, the lie that says we can make real closeness and connection happen by simply learning and applying the best intimacy-growing techniques, and/or by just opening up. Or as many pop culture figures have expressed this popular love lie: "I'm gonna make you love me!"

A Predictable Predicament

If online marriage experts disagree about how to make a truly satisfying emotional connection happen, marketers are more than happy to step into this gap. Their message about real closeness and connection in marriage is that you can make it happen through the regular application of the right romantic products:

- Greeting cards to commemorate anniversaries and other romantic milestones
- Flowers, candy, and other red, heart-shaped gifts
- Sexy underthings for her (and, increasingly, for him!)
- The right perfume for her or aftershave for him
- A feng shui makeover for your bedroom
- Dinners at the right restaurants
- Overnight stays at beautiful getaways
- A gym membership to lose unsightly love handles and bulk up on the kinds of muscles that make women faint
- Drugs that chemically increase love (or at least lust)

If some inventive entrepreneur came up with a pill or injection that would guarantee a rapid rise in romance and intimacy, there would probably be many desperate buyers.

But can these products and other efforts really increase the closeness and connection in your marriage? For decades, this question has played out in the world of popular music. On one side are popular songs claiming one partner can compel the other's affection. This was the case being made back in 1968 when Diana Ross and the Supremes got together with the Temptations for their big hit "I'm Gonna Make You Love Me." The Jayhawks made a similar argument in their song of the same title, featured on the *Dawson's Creek* TV show, promising that love could last forever, that a couple could stay together "for a million years."[1] On the opposite side of the debate, artists including Adele, George Michael, Bonnie Raitt, and dozens of others have recorded or performed a song reaching the opposite conclusion: "I Can't Make You Love Me," which includes the strong statement, "You can't make your heart feel something it won't."

While we've always appreciated the music of the Supremes and the Temptations, we're not so sure about their theology of love. We think we're going to side with Bonnie Raitt and company this time around. While it's great to sing about how one person can make another person feel deeper love, our experience shows the truth lies more in the latter song. While sad, we think it's more accurate to acknowledge we can't make another person love us more deeply.

In love and in faith, human beings exhibit free will. God won't make humans love Him, nor can humans force others to love them. You can't arm wrestle someone into experiencing true emotions. You can't force intimacy.

But there is good news. Our decades of experience with men and women have yielded one enormous gem of wisdom. While you can't force marital bonding by making someone love you, two people can do something powerful together that can greatly increase the odds of making closeness and connection flourish and deepen. We'll tell you our secret in just a moment, but first, another quiz!

Closeness and Connection Self-Assessment

How close are you and your spouse? How close do you want to be? And what are *you* doing to help the two of you grow closer together? Assess your own intimacy quotient by answering the following five questions.

1. On a scale of 1 to 10, how would you describe the level of closeness and connection in your marriage right now?

    1   2   3   4   5   6   7   8   9   10
    Disconnected   Very Close

2. On a scale of 1 to 10, how would you describe your own level of being open to deeper closeness and connection with your partner right now?

    1   2   3   4   5   6   7   8   9   10
    Closed   Open

3. On a scale of 1 to 10, how would you describe your partner's level of being open to deeper closeness and connection with you right now?

    1   2   3   4   5   6   7   8   9   10
    Closed   Open

4. Do you feel your relationship is safe and secure enough that you can reveal your deepest feelings to your spouse?

    1   2   3   4   5   6   7   8   9   10
    Unsafe   Safe

5. Does your spouse feel your relationship is safe and
   secure enough that they can reveal their deepest
   feelings to you?

1	2	3	4	5	6	7	8	9	10
Unsafe									Safe

The Solution

You can't make your partner love you. Sorry about that, Supremes!
You can't force intimacy to happen. Too bad, Temptations!

Here's what you can do: create a safe and secure place where two
people can grow in connection and affection. Marriage provides
the optimal experience to fulfill one of our heart's deepest desires:
to be unconditionally accepted and connected. This ideally means
to develop a real friendship where we deeply know and are known.

The truth, though, is that even under the best circumstances,
opening up enough to be intimate is always risky. Whether it is
the risk of being judged, criticized, betrayed, abandoned, humili-
ated, met with indifference, or an almost endless array of ways to
be hurt, letting someone really know us is dangerous.

In fact, probably the riskiest decision anyone can make is to
truly care. As soon as you care, everything matters. It's far safer
to stay distant and indifferent. The rub is that from the risk-free
zone of physical and emotional separateness, our longing to feel
close and connected can never be satisfied! So what's the solution?

Since the essence of satisfying closeness is actually an "open
heart to open heart" connection, most people we know attempt
to overcome this dilemma with one of two strategies: They either
learn tools and techniques to try to create more closeness and connection, or they find ways to become more open. We find both
approaches to be unnecessarily hard, unsatisfying, and commonly
ineffective.

The alternative is both simple and profound but unfortunately is rarely identified as the primary strategy and goal for creating intimacy. We recommend placing maximum effort and energy into making your marriage safe and secure! Intimacy can flourish when people feel safe and secure, so your objective should not be on making intimacy happen, or getting open, but in creating the kind of safe, secure, loving environment where closeness can thrive.

You've probably seen commercials from companies that say, "Safety is job one." You need to apply this motto to your marriage.

If we want to experience greater intimacy, make sure safety is job one.

If we want our love to grow deeper, make sure safety is job one.

Once again, the principles that govern our relationship with God also govern our love life. As John writes in his epistle: "There is no fear in love, but perfect love casts out fear. For fear has to do with punishment, and whoever fears has not been perfected in love" (1 John 4:18). Perfect love will feel like the safest place on earth.

So what do we mean when we claim security and safety are prerequisites of intimacy and deep love? It's simple. We mean that men and women are much more likely to entrust and open their hearts to each other when they know their hearts will be cared for. This kind of safe, secure care is shown when two people can make these comments about their relationship:

- "I know my partner cares about me."
- "My feelings, thoughts, concerns, and fears matter to my partner."
- "We honor one another, both when we are together and when we are apart."
- "Our personal differences are allowed, valued, and celebrated."

- "Each one of us does our part to build trust in our relationship day by day."
- "We are close, but each one of us can have space if we want it or need it."
- "Although on occasion we may express anger toward one another, our anger is not out of control or dangerous."
- "Although on occasion we may hurt each other, that is never our intention, and we seek forgiveness and healing after any unintended blowups."
- "When we talk and share our feelings about complex subjects, I don't feel judged. Rather I feel understood and cared for."
- "We really feel like partners who are walking alongside each other in the journey of life, not roommates, business partners, or enemy combatants."
- "I know that I can be open, honest, and vulnerable with my spouse because my thoughts, feelings, and comments will be understood and treated with respect."

Why Is Safety and Security Essential?

Why are these conditions so important? Why do we say they are a prerequisite to intimacy? Why do we promise that if you create a safe and secure space, closeness and connection will flourish?

It's because the heart is the center of our life and our relationships. When our heart feels safe, it naturally opens. But when our heart feels fear or senses a threat, it closes down. Think again of the roly-poly bugs we discussed in chapter 3. Good luck having a good conversation when one or both of you have closed up tight like a roly-poly.

When a person experiences fear, that emotion sets in motion a chain reaction. At the very least, fear breeds caution. At its worst, fear can close a heart down. Either condition hinders having a satisfying connection with your spouse.

Contrast the residual impact of this fear with the long-term impact of safety. When a person feels safe, this sets in motion an entirely different chain of reactions: more comfort, greater openness, more soul-searching honesty, and more openhearted vulnerability.

So let's take this one step further and show how these conditions relate to our model of a healthy marriage. First, we'll define the concepts of security and safety, and then we'll show how they fit in our model.

We define security as the confidence that you can count on your spouse to be there with you and for you in good times and bad, to protect all that is valuable and vulnerable in your relationship, and that your spouse can know he or she can count on you to do the same. Sound familiar?

HEALTHY MARRIAGE MODEL

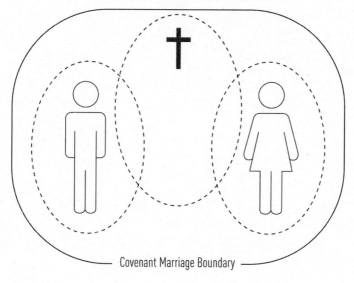

Covenant Marriage Boundary

The outer circle of our model represents our promise/vow to protect the integrity and well-being of our relationship. The primary purpose of that covenant is to create a secure environment for both people to live within.

Safety takes things to another level. We define safety as feeling unconditionally loved and accepted as an imperfect person in the process of healing and growing. This includes knowing that I will be completely respected and protected physically, mentally, spiritually, *and* emotionally. Beyond knowing I can count on you to protect our relationship, safety comes from knowing I can count on you to be there with me, and for me, *as a person.*

HEALTHY MARRIAGE MODEL

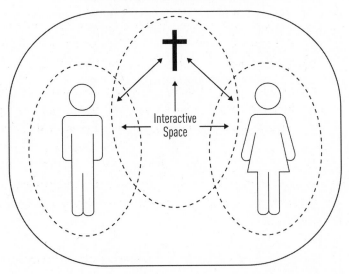

This includes knowing I can move in and out of the inner circle and allow myself to be deeply known—without fear! I don't have to be self-conscious, watching my back (or anything else for that matter), and am able to just be who I am, warts and wrinkles and all. Again, this is the essence of unconditional love and acceptance.

Is Your Marriage a Safe Space?

Think for a moment about the safety level of your marriage. Is your marriage a safe space?

- You can feel safe emotionally (the two of you believe your heart is safe in the other's hands, and the two of you can be honest and vulnerable with each other).

- You can feel safe physically (neither of you fears being hit, slapped, having your body disrespected in any way, or engaged at times or in ways you don't prefer).

- You can feel safe mentally (knowing that you can share thoughts and ideas without fear of humiliation and ridicule, even if it's a poorly thought through idea or comment).

- You can feel safe spiritually (being able to vulnerably pray together, share your beliefs and your unique journey of spiritual growth, and even be open together in the presence of God).

Think about your marriage as you ask yourself the following questions. These are some of the questions we ask couples to answer at our intensives.

- Are there times when you feel unsafe in your marriage, either physically or emotionally?
- Have you ever felt physically threatened?
- Have you ever felt like your spouse either dismissed your emotions or turned them against you?

Think about what's happening between the two of you when those unsafe feelings start to emerge.

- Can you remember what happens between you, or what statement causes things to become unsafe?
- Are there behaviors or practices your spouse engages in that make you feel unsafe in the relationship?

The next question may be even more difficult and more important to answer.

- Are there behaviors or practices that you engage in that make your partner feel unsafe in the relationship?

Take some time to wrestle with this question. Take a walk down memory lane and see if your past behaviors have created an unsafe atmosphere for your partner.

- Have you ever been in a conversation when you felt your partner close down, back off, or walk away? Was there something you did that contributed to that happening?
- Have you ever closed down, backed off, or walked away?

We ask all these questions because safety can be an elusive quality. Many couples don't appreciate it until it's gone, but then some can't figure out where it went or how to get it back.

We suspect that most of the people reading this book have never thought about or never clearly articulated what it is that causes them to be uneasy or cautious and thus to close up. But if the two of you are ever going to figure out how to create a safe place in your relationship to grow a more satisfying closeness and connection, you are going to need to start figuring this out and communicating it to each other.

In the case of Randy and Becky's marriage, safety never was job one. Both were careless. Both uttered cold, thoughtless words. Both committed heartless deeds. They're not bad people—at times they're just a little insensitive and somewhat self-centered after so many years of living alone. Their careless words and actions made each other feel cautious and gradually close down their hearts.

They realize that now, and they want to know what they can do to make their marriage the safest place it can be. In situations like that, we encourage couples to follow our two rules for safe conversations.

Two Rules for Safe Conversations

Listen

For many couples, conversations are a major source of fear and defensiveness. Conversations that start out bland but end up explosive can scare one or more partners from trying to talk. Have you ever engaged in these behaviors during a conversation with your spouse?

- Argued or defended yourself rather than listened
- Laughed at or made fun of something your partner said
- Allowed distractions (your smartphone, the television, your own thoughts) to prevent you from hearing and understanding your partner's words
- Rushed the discussion along because you felt you had more important things to do
- Resurrected past problems from a year or a decade ago

These rhetorical tricks are nonstarters for safe conversations. After all, you're not in a debate club or a political rally. You're talking to your beloved life partner!

Practice listening instead of responding. Prove you've listened by telling your partner, "Here's what I hear you saying." Make it your goal to understand, not to explain or defend. Work on being emotionally present with your spouse so he or she can feel you're really listening instead of trying to change or critique how the other feels.

Choose the Right Setting

Often couples' conversations go off track right away because they don't take place in a manner or environment that both of you find comfortable and safe. You may feel comfortable discussing deep topics while jogging or cooking, but your partner may need to sit down across from you and look into your eyes to be able to feel connected.

We recommend the two of you talk about talking, focusing on the setting that gives you the greatest opportunity for successful conversation. We learned this the hard way, starting conversations with our wives that quickly went south because we failed to properly prepare an environment where we were both comfortable. Setting, environment, and time of day are crucial components of successful conversations. The two of you can vastly increase your conversational competence by setting the stage for safe and meaningful discussions.

Talk together about these important environmental concerns:

- What factors make each of you feel most comfortable when talking about important issues? If you could design a perfect scenario for a safe and intimate conversation, what would it look like? How does that differ, if at all, from your spouse?

- Which setting is the best for good conversation? In the kitchen over dinner, or out to dinner at a restaurant? In the living room or in the bedroom? Or should you head for the great outdoors, talking on your porch or on a park bench? Or are you like some couples who prefer talking while driving?

- What time of the day is best for you? One of you may be an early riser and the other a night owl, but the two of you can still find a way to agree on a good time for your important conversations.

- How long? Some conversations are like flowers: fragrant for a while but then they quickly go bad. Before you start a new conversation, negotiate a time frame. Is this a simple ten-minute talk about a few mundane matters, or is this a potentially more challenging two-hour discussion of an important but troubling issue? Scope it out before you start and renegotiate along the way if you need to.

- Dissenting opinions? Find out how each of you feels about the other person expressing disagreements or negative viewpoints. The two of you don't have to totally agree on everything, but some people don't know how to disagree in an agreeable manner. Give each other space to hear each other out and to express differing viewpoints without fear of judgment or retribution.

Conversations that end poorly often started out poorly, but if the two of you can learn to negotiate these issues of place, timing, and goals, your rate of successful conversations will soar to new heights.

Building Trust

You can be the world's greatest conversationalists, but if your relationship does not rest on a solid foundation of trust, its safety and security will be endangered. Trust issues are common and can be very complicated. But if safety is your goal, you will continually work to earn and re-earn your partner's trust, because trust with humans is never earned once and for all. We're all capable of becoming untrustworthy in any moment. Therefore, rather than trying to get your spouse to trust you, we encourage you to make your goal to be as close to fully trustworthy as possible.

So what is being trustworthy, and why is trust so easy to lose? When you are trustworthy, you demonstrate by everything you say and do that you fully understand how valuable and vulnerable the other person truly is. Every human being is a child of the Most High God and therefore is of incalculable value. At the same time, like all things of high value, people can be easily damaged and devalued. You are trustworthy to the degree that all of that value and vulnerability are reflected in what you do and say. To any degree you lose sight of that reality, even for a moment, you are less trustworthy.

This was a big *aha* for me (Bob). I used to regularly ask and expect Jenni to trust me. After all, I cared for her and she knew my basic heart and intent were good. Unconsciously, I figured the longer we were together, the more that trust should grow and become a given.

However, God finally helped me see that, as a flawed human being, I am wired to be self-focused. For example, if by some weird fluke of circumstance we both slam our fingers in the door simultaneously, I am wired to focus more on my finger than Jenni's. In that moment I'm thinking more about me than I am about her. Not that I don't care, but I'm *feeling* my pain! And anytime I'm thinking more about me, I'm not fully trustworthy to Jenni, and I'm capable of inadvertently hurting her.

She's too valuable for me to accept that, even by accident. But being a mere mortal, I know it's possible. Therefore, I never ask Jenni to trust me anymore. I want her always protected and safe. Instead of trying to *get her* to trust, I focus all my efforts on *being* trustworthy. I count on Jenni to carefully discern how safe I seem to her in any given moment. In fact, I love her so much I'd rather she err on the side of overreacting and staying safe than under-reacting and getting hurt.

With that attitude, do you think she experiences me as more or less safe than before? I promise you, it's a game changer.

We think of trust as a big, solid house that provides the structure and safety love needs to grow. Trust becomes a shelter in which both of you can relax as you openly and intimately share your lives together. Think of trust as a relational sanctuary, a safe harbor, or a big, comfy easy chair that you long to come home to.

Why is trust so important? Opening yourself up to another person and sharing your deepest loves, concerns, and secrets always involves an element of risk. Will you be hurt? Will you be ridiculed? Will you be rejected? If you don't feel your heart is in safe hands, you won't trust it to another.

Trust is a two-way street. We recommend you commit yourself to being trustworthy and demonstrate your trustworthiness through your behavior and your care. We also recommend, prior to allowing access to your valuable, vulnerable parts, you expect your partner to be trustworthy toward you.

If trust has been broken by emotional and/or sexual unfaithfulness, safety is at risk. The fracturing of trust that results from infidelity is difficult to overcome, but it can be done with commitment, grace, love, and God's mercy. It does require a fair amount of effort and intention, but we've watched hundreds of couples work together with the Lord to resurrect a great marriage out of the devastation of an affair.

Learning to Love

Randy and Becky spent decades preparing themselves for successful careers. In the last year, they've invested themselves with equal passion in building a successful marriage.

They've made some exciting changes in their daily lives. For one thing, they are now placing a higher priority on setting aside time to be with each other instead of waiting and hoping for a window of time to open up somewhere in their overbooked calendars. They have weekly date nights, and on the weekends, together they're using those athletic clothes that sat in their closets for so long.

They're spending a minimum of ten minutes a day talking to each other without agendas or distractions. Usually they talk right after they both get home from work and change their clothes. They unwind from the day in each other's loving presence, getting serious when they need to and laughing loudly together when the moment strikes them.

During a series of longer weekend conversations, they talked about what safety means to them. They explored what makes them feel safe or unsafe. Those talks revolutionized the way they talk and the way they treat each other.

The women in Becky's Bible study and the men in Randy's small group can see that the marriage is different. They can tell these two aren't stuck anymore.

Exercises for Making Safety Job One

Many husbands and wives sincerely want to make their marriages safe places in all aspects (physically, mentally, spiritually, and emotionally), but some just don't know how. Here are our exercises for creating a safe environment where intimacy can flourish.

Reflect and Discuss

We asked some important questions in this chapter about safety and intimacy. Start by devoting some time to looking in the mirror as you answer the following three questions. Then, after both of you have come up with your best answers, sit down and compare notes.

What do I do, or not do, that makes my spouse feel less safe in our marriage?

What do I do, or not do, that makes me feel less safe in our marriage?

What can I do to make my marriage feel safer for my spouse and for me?

Make a Safety Action Plan

Come up with a plan to convert your answers to the questions into two or three specific actions you can start taking immediately to increase the safety level in your marriage.

Talk About Fear Versus Safety

In this chapter we talked about how God designed us to be open and intimate. That's our ideal default setting and requires the least amount of energy to maintain. But when we feel unsafe, we close up and become protected and disconnected.

Many men and women invest much energy into trying to make openness and intimacy happen in their marriage. Some try to force it. But as we've seen, growing intimacy is a by-product of trust and safety. There are basically two directions relationships can go:

1. Toward More Safety and Security → Openness → Close and Connected
2. Toward Less Safety → Closing Up → Distance and Disconnection

Talk together about the direction things have gone in the past and the direction you want them to go in the future. Compare notes about the times you've been less safe and closed down, and about the times you've felt safe and opened up. What did these experiences feel like inside? How did they impact your relationship?

Recognize Your Behaviors

Safety often comes down to behaviors. A particular word or action can cause hearts to close. Take a good look at this list and note any behaviors you have engaged in. Commit to changing your actions and seeking forgiveness for failing to make safety job one in the past.

Ask yourself these safety questions:

1. What do I do, or not do, that makes my spouse feel less safe in our marriage? Put a check mark by any of the behaviors you have engaged in. Put a plus sign by those behaviors that you regularly engage in.

   - Angry outbursts
   - Threats (violence, leaving, finances, divorce, etc.)
   - Ignoring issues
   - Withdrawal (not addressing issues now or later)
   - Sarcastic humor (without regard for the other's feelings)

- Stating or implying, "Your feelings are wrong/
irrelevant/stupid."
- Criticizing

2. What do I do, or not do, that makes me feel less safe in our
marriage? Put a check mark by any of the behaviors you
have engaged in. Put a plus sign by those behaviors that
you regularly engage in.

- I have weak boundaries, or no boundaries that I
enforce.
- I ignore, judge, dismiss, or criticize my own feelings.
- I stay in a conversation/argument when I feel unsafe,
which only makes me feel worse.
- I ignore or don't address issues I have concerns or
feelings about.
- I fail to control my anger.
- I weaken trust by not following through on my
promises and commitments.

3. What can I do to make my marriage feel safer for me and
my spouse? See what you can come up with.

LOVE LIE #8:

"YOUR LOVE IS DRIVING ME CRAZY!"

Geoff grew up in a home where emotions were kept under tight control. Feelings were parceled out in small doses; otherwise people might be overwhelmed by what his parents called "rampant emotionalism."

Expressing too much spontaneous thankfulness for a great birthday present was considered "unseemly."

Showing too much grief at a funeral for a close relative was deemed "weak."

Even laughing too much at a hilarious joke could be called "out of control."

But Geoff had plenty of strong feelings and was actually more comfortable with them than his parents were, so he frequently felt stifled by his family. He liked feelings of love and passion and longed for greater freedom of emotional expression with whatever woman would be his wife. He more than met his match when he fell head over heels for Michelle, who grew up amid an emotional free-for-all.

You never knew how Michelle's dad was going to show up on any particular day. Would it be the gregarious jokester? The grumpy old man complaining about the latest news headline? Or would he be "resting" and "not able to see anyone right now"?

Geoff didn't give Michelle's dad too much thought, but he sure did appreciate how alive Michelle seemed. She was passionate about everything. Compared to his family, she was incredibly interesting and colorful! She could erupt into tears multiple times during a good romantic movie. And sometimes after Geoff said something kind and loving to her, she would smile really big and say, "Oh, that's the sweetest thing anyone ever said to me." Michelle also cried during worship services at church. Geoff thought this was better than the cold Lutheranism of his youth.

Geoff couldn't believe his fortune in finding someone who experienced everything—including her love for him—with such depth of feeling. Their romance developed rapidly, they married, and they got busy having a family.

But within a month of their honeymoon, Geoff was getting worried about Michelle's combustibility. Some days were like the Fourth of July, with fireworks exploding here and there. Other days were more like waterworks, with Michelle's eyes tear-filled over some sorrow weighing heavily on her heart.

Things grew even crazier when she was pregnant with their first boy. Things didn't calm down much during the next *four* pregnancies—all girls.

Over time, Geoff began to feel he was drowning in a house overflowing with feminine emotion. Michelle's emotions dominated the mood of the entire household. But to Michelle, the marriage was an emotional desert. She felt Geoff was aloof, remote, or "emotionally constipated." She told one close girlfriend she believed Geoff might be autistic. She could never understand why he repeatedly failed to be emotionally there for her amid life's normal ups and downs.

When they came to one of our intensives, Michelle talked and cried as she detailed her many trials and tribulations. Geoff was quiet unless we asked him a question. His eyes had the look of a soldier who had survived tours in Iraq but had brought home a case of post-traumatic stress disorder (PTSD).

They'd been married twelve years, and most of the last decade had been an increasingly frustrating standoff between what he saw as emotional chaos and what she saw as his lack of interest and care.

That explains how Geoff embraced Love Lie #8: "Your love is driving me crazy!" The essence of this lie is simple: One partner believes the other partner's emotions are destabilizing and destructive for the relationship and believes the best way to fix things is to have one's feelings controlled, restrained, or eliminated.

Here's how Geoff explained it to us in the intensive: "I feel like Michelle's powerful emotions need to be contained or somehow overcome if our marriage is to survive."

But before Geoff had even finished his sentence, Michelle interrupted, amid sobs, "What kind of love is it when you can't feel a thing?" she asked, as she complained about having her feelings judged, dismissed, and called "stupid."

Feelings and Freak-Outs

Both Geoff and Michelle are emotional people, but their troubled relationship shows that no two people experience or act upon their emotions in exactly the same ways. They experience emotions in such different ways that Michelle often concludes Geoff has no emotions. But that's not fair. As we often find in marriages like theirs, the quieter and more reserved partner typically has deep feelings but is cautious about expressing them in such an emotionally volatile environment.

When they were dating, Geoff was attracted to Michelle's emotional depth and complexity. She was attracted to what she saw as Geoff's stability. During those early days she repeatedly told him, "You are my rock." He liked that.

But these several years later, Geoff is now fearful about the harm he believes Michelle's unbridled emotions and regular outbursts are causing their marriage and family. He was taught to distrust strong emotions, and he is now far more inclined to agree.

Meanwhile, Michelle no longer refers to Geoff as her rock. Instead, she describes him to her two closest girlfriends as "a wet blanket on my heart" or as having as many feelings as a "big boulder." The big boulder comparison is doubly troubling to Geoff, who resents being told he has no feelings and also struggles to control his weight.

From Geoff's perspective, the problems in their marriage stem not from his lack of emotional expression but from what he considers Michelle's emotional excesses and her inability or lack of interest in reining in her outbursts. "These emotions are tearing us apart," he says. "They're destroying me and destroying us."

When we see couples like Geoff and Michelle, it's sad to see the destruction their differing views of emotion, their emotional disconnect, and their periodic outbursts have caused. Based on his background, it's no wonder Geoff feels Michelle's emotions are dangerous, and it explains his deep desire to turn down the volume and heat in their relationship. Geoff believes it would be better for the two of them to be distant and unemotional than to be dangerously emotional and unstable.

Having grown up containing his emotions, Geoff has used this skill to his benefit at work. In big meetings where other company executives sometimes derail progress with rants or outbursts, Geoff is admired as the calm, mature adult in the room. "You're our rudder in the storm," a coworker told him after one particularly boisterous meeting. Such experiences at work convinced Geoff even more that some kind of emotional control with Michelle would bring the same benefits at home.

We could see for ourselves how powerful Michelle's emotions were. She was fairly vocal with her comments, and her tears flowed easily. Her own frustration with Geoff was clear, and once we even had to ask her not to attack Geoff for his supposed lack of feelings. It was perfectly clear how Michelle felt about Geoff's emotional absence.

At one point, though, we asked Geoff how he felt when Michelle would get so frustrated with him. He began sobbing and had to take a minute or two to regain control of himself before he could talk. "It hurts," he said, wiping away tears. "It really hurts."

We could see why Geoff would embrace Love Lie #8. Michelle's love *was* driving Geoff crazy. At times, Geoff even fantasizes about a miracle pill, a medical procedure, or a counseling session that could reduce, stabilize, or even eliminate Michelle's emotions.

More Than a Feeling

These reactions are understandable, and Geoff is not alone. Many spouses—often men—feel they're the victims of supersize emotions. But is containment and control the best, or only, solution? Do we need to neuter our spouses so they are less difficult or threatening?

We don't think so. Emotional expression can be very destructive, but seeking to downsize emotions or do away with them altogether isn't the answer. Life just wouldn't be life without them. At least not human life.

The fact is, God created emotions. He has a grand purpose in our complicated feelings. Our emotions are a valuable source of insight and information into our hearts. By design, emotions are informers. They give us a window into what is going on inside us. They are not only valuable; they are essential.

Jesus experienced powerful emotions. In the shortest verse in the Bible, John tells us, "Jesus wept" (John 11:35). If you look at this brief verse in context, you can see that Jesus is grieving over the recent death of his friend Lazarus. Later in the same chapter of John, Jesus performs one of his many miracles by raising Lazarus from the dead. The fascinating thing about all this is that Jesus deeply grieved his friend's death even though he knew he would soon raise him from the dead.

Apparently, Jesus didn't think His intense emotions were a waste of time. He obviously loved Lazarus deeply! Feeling and expressing His deep sorrow was evidence of that. Perhaps Jesus was also crying not for Lazarus alone but for all people who have been touched by sorrow. In both cases, we see the feeling and expression as affirming both His and our humanity.

King David was also a man of strong feelings. In Psalm 30, David describes the up-and-down feelings he has, depending on whether he perceives God to be present or absent:

When I felt secure, I said,
   "I will never be shaken."
LORD, when you favored me,
   you made my royal mountain stand firm;
but when you hid your face,
   I was dismayed.
PSALM 30:6-7, NIV

But when David thinks back and remembers everything he has come through, he concludes on a more positive note:

> You have turned for me my mourning into dancing;
>   you have loosed my sackcloth and clothed me with
>   gladness.
>
> PSALM 30:11

He expresses similar sentiments when he says:

> Weeping may last for the night,
>   But a shout of joy comes in the morning.
>
> PSALM 30:5, NASB

Geoff often finds himself unable to comprehend why Michelle reacts the way she does and as strongly as she does. He considers some of her outbursts unreal because they seem to have no relationship to external realities. He thinks they're overreactions to scenarios she imagines in her head.

But we give emotions more credit than that. They're incredibly important because they're a great source of heart data. God created emotions to inform us about the condition of our hearts; they actually reveal the state of a person's heart better than other indicators. That's part of the reason we say emotions are morally neutral and should be listened to rather than judged.

Geoff grew up believing there are "good" emotions we can enjoy and "bad" emotions we had better keep under wraps. His experiences with Michelle have only strengthened his understanding of good and bad emotions. The good ones are those that feel good and don't explode in his face. The bad ones cause him to close up inside and flee for the exits.

Many people actually agree with Geoff's policy of declaring some emotions good while others are bad, or at least inconvenient. Who hasn't heard someone being told:

"Relax! Stop crying."

"Just get over it!"

"You're too emotional."

"You have no good reason to be mad."

We have news for Geoff. Emotions are neither good nor bad. We acknowledge that some emotions can have a destructive impact, but that's not the fault of the emotions themselves. Destruction has more to do with how we use our emotions against others or how we allow them to fuel self-destructive behavior.

In our intensives with couples who are struggling with emotions (both their own and their spouses'), we try to help them better understand God's design and purpose for emotions. With that understanding in place, we help them learn ways to interpret, manage, and utilize these essential indicators in order to assure both people, and their relationship, are well cared for.

As we told Geoff: "Geoff, one of your jobs—and it's going to be a hard job—is to listen to Michelle's heart and care about how she feels, without taking responsibility for her feelings. You want to balance this with caring about how you feel too. Both of you matter, and both hearts matter. So it may include setting some healthy boundaries or ground rules to assure neither of you get hurt.

"This may seem impossible or inconceivable now, but your job over the long term is to learn to be fully present with Michelle and thus present with her emotions, regardless of whether they seem to be 'good' or 'bad' feelings. This will let her know that you truly care about her because you care about how she feels. It doesn't require you to feel the same nor to do exactly what she wants. Generally, when someone believes their feelings matter to another, they feel loved, even when the feelings seem irrational! And as we said a moment ago, it also does not require accepting or indulging hurtful behavior."

Couples like Geoff and Michelle also need to realize that being one in marriage doesn't mean both partners must feel the same thing. That will never happen. Rather, oneness means oneness of purpose, oneness in love for each other. It doesn't mean emotional similarity or uniformity.

Achieving this kind of unity is not easy, especially when some couples seem to be stuck because they don't know what to do with their many emotions. What does Geoff do when Michelle is hurting? He gets scared and runs. These feelings seem dangerous to him. Not because he doesn't care but because he's freaking out. What does Michelle do when Geoff is running away at a million miles an hour? She admitted to us that she typically raises her voice even louder. Sometimes she follows him so that he hears her loud and clear.

Their lack of appreciation of God's design and purpose for emotions, combined with two very different emotional styles and a complete lack of emotional strategy and skill, has created their unstable and dangerous emotional environment. Both of them are convinced their partner isn't feeling things accurately or appropriately, and both are working overtime to change how the other person feels and expresses emotions.

Our plea to these emotionally traumatized couples is simple: Don't run. Don't hide. Don't try to eliminate or manipulate your partner's feelings. Rather, work with your partner to create a safe and effective way to understand, care, and make good use of one of God's primary sources of relational data.

That's what we told Geoff, who immediately asked us, "How in the world do we make these feelings more manageable? I would love to do that!"

We have the answer Geoff and so many other couples need. We call it Heart Talk, and it's one of the most powerful marriage tools we give the couples we work with.

But first, another assessment!

Assessing Your Relationship's Emotional Health

1. I view unpleasant and/or intense feelings as negative, bad, or wrong.

1	2	3	4	5	6	7	8	9	10
Never				Sometimes					Always

2. My spouse's feelings are understood and accepted by me.

1	2	3	4	5	6	7	8	9	10
Never				Sometimes					Always

3. My feelings are understood and accepted by my spouse.

1	2	3	4	5	6	7	8	9	10
Never				Sometimes					Always

4. When we are both experiencing strong feelings, I believe I have to choose between caring about mine or caring about my spouse's.

1	2	3	4	5	6	7	8	9	10
Never				Sometimes					Always

5. I see feelings as the primary communication substance for creating intimate closeness and connection.

1	2	3	4	5	6	7	8	9	10
Never				Sometimes					Always

Talking Heart to Heart

Here's our prescription for combating Love Lie #8. Instead of driving each other crazy, Michelle and Geoff need to have a good, long talk, the kind of deep, heart-to-heart talk they may not have shared in a decade or more.

We call this special conversation Heart Talk. We used to call it Emotional Communication. There are many versions of this style of communication around, and each version has a different name. However, we've been working for years to refine our approach and have created the simplest, easiest-to-use format we know of. Whatever you call it, Michelle and Geoff desperately need it.

The structure and goals of Heart Talk are simple, but the execution proves difficult for some couples due to stubborn old habits of communication they've gotten used to. The primary objective in a Heart Talk is for each person to be able to share how he or she feels about something and to end up feeling really understood, accepted, and cared for.

The above outcome can feel pretty elusive at times when strong feelings are present for a variety of reasons. As in the case of Geoff and Michelle, many couples possess different emotional styles, they have differing views on the value of certain emotions, and they lack a proven method of communicating about feelings that can set them up to succeed relationally. When they get upset, everyone's talking and no one's really listening. Heart Talk provides a solution for all of those challenges.

The basics of Heart Talk are that one of you talks about something that's on your heart while the other listens and tries to understand. That's it. One person shares, the other tries to empathize and "get" what that partner is feeling. Remember, the underlying emotions have to be the key focus for both so that each person ends up feeling heard and cared for. When done well, the couple ends up feeling close and connected. And taking turns is absolutely essential so that neither spouse is neglected or overshadowed.

Sounds simple, doesn't it? But for Geoff and Michelle, this kind of deep sharing disappeared long ago. They still talk. Most married couples do. But most of the talking couples do isn't Heart Talk. When we're not arguing, most of the time we have work conversations designed to address logistics and get something done.

We'll clarify what we mean by Heart Talk by contrasting it with a couple of other common forms of conversations couples engage in every day.

Heart Talk and Work Talk

Conversation is essential for a successful marriage. We've described conversation as the mortar that holds a marriage together, or as the vital lifeblood that flows through a successful relationship. Now let's take a look at the two types of communication that help build relationships: Heart Talk and Work Talk.

There are actually many valid types of communication, and each one drives toward a different objective. For instance, debate is a powerful communication style that many use, and some are trained in it and even use it in competition. Debate typically drives toward the goal of winning or persuading, which in the right hands can be used to help accomplish great things. Debate, however, is rarely a key to growing a great marriage.

Another commonly used type of conversation is one we'll call small talk. We all know this one, but unfortunately some judge it as meaningless chatter. But we understand that small talk is really designed to make a connection with someone. Talking about the weather, or whatever, can easily help bridge the gap between me and you and make a basic connection happen.

Over the years, though, we've noticed that couples who have thriving marriages skillfully use two very specific styles of communication. One type is what we call Work Talk, which is designed to get stuff done. For our lives to succeed, there is a never-ending array of logistics that need attention, things like:

"Hey, honey, how are we going to pick up your car from the garage?"

"Hey, honey, do you think you would have any time this weekend to help me clean out the hall closet?"

Additionally, problems, differences, and numerous other challenges occur regularly. Work Talk is the ideal method to use for overcoming issues and conflict. When done well, it leads to a satisfying sense of accomplishment. We'll explore Work Talk in the next chapter.

Heart Talk is a whole different animal. Heart Talk is not about logistics, plans, or catching up. It's not about resolving conflicts or managing differences. It's about sharing the deepest part of yourself with another person. As previously stated, the substance of Heart Talk is feelings; the goal of Heart Talk is closeness and intimacy. When done well, it leads to a profound experience of connection and bonding.

If your goal as a couple is to be great business partners, Heart Talk is optional. However, if your goal is to feel genuinely close and connected, Heart Talk is the most important kind of conversation husbands and wives can have. When everything is smooth and relaxed, Heart Talk commonly happens without much thought. But our experience reveals that when strong feelings enter the scene, we commonly need a little help. Let us show you the basics so that when needed, you have a road map to assure your success.

Rules of the Road: Sharing, Caring, and Understanding

When discussing matters of the heart, we encourage couples to remember that safety is job one. Don't forget the admonition in Proverbs 4:23 to guard your heart above all else. These conversations can become some of the most meaningful and bonding connections in your marriage, although sharing how you feel about something instantly creates vulnerability. If a spouse gets hurt as a result of opening up, the likelihood of that person returning for more conversation drops dramatically.

That's why our simplified emotional communication model is a three-step process that accounts for that vulnerability. Our process is based on the acronym ICU, which most people connect with an intensive care unit in a hospital, where highly vulnerable patients are given the highest degree of attention and care. Since you will be discussing matters of the heart, we want you to create your own marital ICU, with a mutual commitment to make sure you both proceed with tremendous care and respect.

With that in mind, the actual first step is for one of you to initiate a conversation. This could be because you have feelings you'd love your spouse to understand and care about, or it could be that you sense your spouse has feelings you'd like to care about, if they're interested in sharing. In the first case it could sound like, "I've got something going on I'd love to talk with you about. Are you open to having a Heart Talk?"

Notice, asking if someone is available is essential for caring for both of you. If your spouse isn't in a place to attend well to your heart, you'd be a careless fool to lay it out there. Respecting yourself requires being thoughtful and careful about when and to whom you open up.

Additionally, if your spouse is not in a good place to listen, trying to force them to do so isn't respectful to them either. In this scenario, you might sense your spouse has a lot going on emotionally, and you want them to know you noticed, and it matters to you. That initiation could sound like this: "Hey, honey, I can see you've got some strong feelings going on. If you're interested in talking, I'm completely available for a Heart Talk."

For this to remain respectful, you must be prepared for them to say, "No" or "Not now."

That should then be followed by, "Okay, if you change your mind and decide you want to talk, just let me know."

In either case, when you begin a Heart Talk you want to be clear about who is starting off as the speaker and who will be the listener. Once that's established, you're ready to proceed.

One of the beauties of our model is we've narrowed down the steps to only three, and they are the exact same steps for both speaker and listener, with only one minor difference.

Step 1: Identify the feelings.
Step 2: Care about the feelings.
Step 3: Understand the feelings.

Each participant does all three. The only difference is that the speaker focuses on his or her own feelings, and the listener focuses on the speaker's feelings. Once the speaker feels heard, understood, and cared for, you switch roles and proceed until both feel heard, understood, and cared for. It's really that simple. Now let's put a little more flesh on the bones so you can really make this work.

In the ideal Heart Talk, the first speaker shares something they have feelings about. You can give some context (what happened, what you heard, etc.), but you focus on what you *felt*.

For example, here's how Michelle could start a Heart Talk about a lunch with her good friend: "I feel so happy and grateful that my friend and I had this wonderful time together, but I'm sad that her son is giving her so many problems."

If Geoff starts as the listener, he attempts to summarize what he heard Michelle say, and he focuses on what she felt. He wants to be tentative, letting Michelle determine whether he heard her heart accurately: "What I hear you saying is that you are both happy and sad about your lunch talk. Is that right?"

She can let him know he understood her correctly, offer a clarification, or just say yes and add more. We recommend that the speaker share in bite-size segments so as not to overwhelm the listener and make it harder for that spouse to remember the important parts. Either at the agreed-upon end time (sometimes people like to decide up front how long this will last), or when the speaker has said what's on his or her heart, the two spouses then switch roles and repeat the process. After getting this green light from Geoff, Michelle shares more details about her experience and feelings.

Things would have gone differently if Geoff had tried to transform this Heart Talk into a Work Talk. For example, he could have responded to Michelle's sadness about her friend's son by recommending a fix in this way: "Well, maybe we could introduce her to the counselor who helped our son so much."

Stop it, Geoff! Michelle is trying to talk to you about her heart. Don't respond by putting on your engineer's hat and trying to solve a problem. Listen to her heart. Understand what she is saying about the woman and her son. That's your priority here. It's your only mission. Your job is to feel, not fix. Remember the goal of Heart Talk is to feel close and connected, not to fix or resolve anything. If a solution to something is needed after both feel heard and cared for, you can switch to Work Talk, which we outline in the next chapter. That's the tool to fix stuff.

Also, things would have gone differently if Michelle had started things off on the wrong foot by saying, "I feel you are the biggest idiot in the universe." True, her sentence starts with the two important words *I feel.* But she's not talking about her feelings here so much as she's reciting a persistent complaint or criticism about Geoff. Michelle forgot that Heart Talk is her chance to talk about *her own feelings and experiences,* not to gripe about Geoff's many alleged misdeeds. When people try these switcheroos in our intensives, we stop them, ask them to start over, and instruct them to talk about their feelings.

If Geoff has become a champion Heart Talker, he will successfully deflect any efforts to take him away from his one and only mission: understanding her heart. He doesn't respond by expressing his opinion or offering a judgment. That could shoot down the whole Heart Talk.

"Remember, Geoff, it's not about you," we say. "It's about her and her feelings. You want her to know that how she feels matters enough to you that you're willing to take the time to know her emotionally."

Here's a table that summarizes the Heart Talk basics and who does what:

HEART TALK

Speaker		Listener
Get in touch with your emotions.		Focus on your spouse's feelings.
Ask for time and give your heart a voice.	<u>I</u>dentify <u>C</u>are <u>U</u>nderstand	Allow your heart to be impacted by their feelings.
Seek to be understood. Express your emotion directly: "When _____ happens, I feel _____."		Demonstrate understanding. Summarize and validate what they felt.

This style of communication can feel a little awkward or unnatural at first, but with some practice that really changes. The benefit is that both of you end up feeling heard, understood, and cared for. If you do need to move into Work Talk, in the next chapter we teach the Seven Steps to a Win-Win. But having a good Heart Talk first can really help. You may have heard the old expression "People don't care what you know until they know you care." Resolving issues is so much easier when neither person is concerned that how they feel won't matter.

Making Heart Talk Work for You

After numerous failed attempts at Heart Talk, Jenni and I (Bob) finally succeeded. I was trained and skilled at using this tool with clients but couldn't seem to make it work at home with the person who mattered most, my wife. Jenni was the one who finally came up with the idea that enabled us to customize our approach to Heart Talk that set up our personal breakthrough.

On her suggestion we packed up our laptops at 6:45 on Wednesday evening and headed to the local library for the first of our regularly scheduled Heart Talks. The talks started promptly at 7:00 p.m., and we allowed ourselves two hours for what became our weekly investment into trying to heal our marriage. At the time, our relationship felt deeply broken.

You might ask why we packed up and went to a library to talk. The surface answer was simple: It worked for us. The sad, underlying answer was that we weren't safe at home! In those days, we finally admitted we lacked self-control. We found it was safer to have our conversation somewhere public so that we'd be less likely to engage in tactics that derail conversations, such as raising our voices at each other or a host of other unfortunate things we gave ourselves permission to say and do. Our outbursts and unkind comments never helped our conversations, so we had to find a neutral venue where external pressures helped prevent us from saying things we might regret later.

Sure, we could have gone to a Starbucks. In fact, we tried, but that was too small and hemmed in. Our library had plenty of room, and you're not supposed to raise your voice there. We appreciated that environment, and the fear of making a public scene and getting kicked out of the library helped us at times where we were tempted to not keep it quiet and polite.

Why the laptops? We finally realized that Jenni's attention deficit disorder (ADD) made it difficult and frustrating for her to fully express herself with short back-and-forth statements. We had to customize Heart Talk to make it work for us. As she spoke, I used my laptop to take down notes, trying hard not to interrupt and knock her off track. There were a couple times when she was really upset, and I typed three pages of notes. Phew! But it worked! And she felt heard, understood, and cared for.

There were a couple of times Jenni hit one of my buttons and I had to call a quick time-out. After a couple of laps around the library, breathing deeply, praying, and practicing my Care Cycle, I was able to return and safely continue the conversation.

We don't have to go to the library anymore. We've actually developed a lot of self-control and are totally committed to maintaining our family ICU. Today each of us cares well for our own heart and the precious heart of our spouse. However, if you need the library, go ahead.

But do I recommend all couples drive down to the library for Heart Talks, or that all husbands do laps when the talks break down? Certainly not. I'm trying to show you what worked for us so that you will be able to find something that works equally well for you. Use our model as a framework to assure the basics are covered. Feel free, though, to customize to fit you and your marriage.

Talking to Connect

Geoff and Michelle are learning how to talk to each other all over again. They spend at least ten minutes every night talking about family issues and logistics, and they check in with each other once or twice every day. They have also scheduled weekly date nights where they take turns doing Heart Talks. On a good night, each one of them gets to share at least one major piece of his or her heart while the other works on understanding.

Michelle's outbursts have not totally stopped, but they are much less frequent, and she's more responsive to Geoff when he signals to her that her comments are hurting or scaring him. And Geoff still runs for the exits every once in a while, but he always makes sure he tries to return to Michelle with an open heart as soon as possible. He's working consistently on becoming a champion Heart Talker, and the prospects look good. There are far fewer explosions in their home and far more moments of loving care and compassion.

"Frankly," Geoff told us, "everything feels pretty good!"

Heart Talk Exercises

Do a Heart Talk Practice Round

You can practice Heart Talk on any issues you'd like to discuss. For couples like Michelle and Geoff, we urge them to start with smaller issues. You can tackle the bigger, more complicated feelings once you get the hang of Heart Talk.

Choose a fun topic like your ideal date night, dream vacation, or something from your bucket list. For example, let's consider your dream vacation. Take turns describing in detail where you would go (warm or cold climate, a particular country, certain time of year, etc.) and what you would do (relax on the beach, ski down a double black diamond, visit the Holy Land, etc.). Practice listening and repeating back what you hear your spouse saying—especially the emotions.

Remember your mission: You are trying to create a heart-to-heart connection. This is not the time to Work Talk—discussing budgeting, childcare, or time frame. The goal is understanding and caring, not resolving or fixing anything. If necessary, that comes later.

If things don't go well during your first Heart Talk session, stop and regroup. You may be able to get back on track right away, but in some cases you may need to wait a day or two before trying again. Utilize what happened in your first session to help you succeed on your second effort. In fact, you can use your unsuccessful attempt at Heart Talk as an effective learning tool to move you toward increased skill and ultimate success. Growth and learning turn a seeming failure into a valuable asset, so relax and just do the best you can.

Review Your Heart Talk

Effective communication moves beyond your spouse's words to the heart and feelings behind his or her words. Have you neglected to validate your spouse's feelings in the past? How do you think that made your spouse feel? If your spouse says he or she feels neglected, don't jump out of your chair and head for the exit, but listen to see what you can learn.

Become even better and more successful in your conversations by discussing your discussions. What can the two of you do differently in order to enhance your ability to listen from your heart to your spouse's heart and feelings? Do Heart Talk well, and you can make a positive and significant change in the quality of communication between the two of you, and these conversations can become a rich source of connection and satisfaction.

Label Hot Topics

Most couples have successful Work Talk and small talk conversations throughout the day. We often don't give ourselves credit for those successes because we hardly pay attention to them. So stop and celebrate the many good talks you have.

The moments that really tend to grab our attention are the colossal conversational meltdowns that leave one or more people uncomfortable or hurt. For many of us, unpleasant conversations are more likely to occur when we're discussing specific topics or when we're under pressure. What topics do you tend to communicate well about and what issues are more likely to make you struggle? What could you both do differently to better set you up for communication success around hot topics or difficult circumstances?

Speak Words of Life
We have talked in this chapter about difficult conversations, but our words are also capable of speaking life into our relationships. This requires that we first recognize the things we find valuable and precious about our mate. What things have you identified? How have you attempted to speak life into your partner by recognizing this value? What are some new ways to demonstrate the value you see in your spouse?

Prayerfully ask the Lord to let you see your spouse through His eyes, to see what He values and feel what He feels. Make note of what you see differently when you look through the Lord's eyes versus what you typically see when looking through your own. Share those new insights with your spouse and celebrate.

Understand Your Buttons
We talked about buttons in chapter 6, as part of your Reactive Cycle. Attempt to explore the early origins of some of your buttons. Don't focus on the marriage but on the experiences and life lessons you had before marriage that made you who you are.

Fears are buttons that are often the result of negative messages written on the "tablets of human hearts" (2 Corinthians 3:3). Can you identify several of the negative messages from your past?

Where did they come from? What does the Lord say about you and these messages today?

Use Heart Talk as your primary communication method when discussing the answers to these questions.

LOVE LIE #9:

YOU WIN SOME, YOU LOSE SOME

"Watch where you're going!" Matt snarled as he turned to face the person who had bumped into him.

"Hey! You're the one who stopped dead in your tracks," the pretty coed said with her own level of snarliness.

Matt and Janet's first meeting sparked interest as well as initial irritation.

"Yeah," Matt told a buddy later in the football locker room. "She was so cute, all riled up and sassy. A real looker, too. Tall, long blonde hair, and blue eyes just blazing at me."

In another locker room across campus, Janet was also telling her teammate about meeting Matt. "He's huge! A linebacker who seemed to think I should recognize his name. I let him know I missed a bunch of games when on the road myself for away volleyball games. It was no surprise that he didn't know my name either."

"So," her friend asked, "will you be seeing him again?"

"Yeah, he asked me to go out with him on Sunday afternoon, the only time we're both free from practices and games."

For the next two years, Matt and Janet dated each other exclusively and found they shared a common approach to resolving conflicts: duke it out until the best man or woman wins. They had come to this conclusion from their experiences growing up.

Matt loved football and learned early on the value of being tough. His father had played professional ball and coached a college team during Matt's growing-up years.

"I remember being in the locker room as a little kid and looking up at all those big, strong guys," Matt told Janet. "They were protective of me as the coach's kid, but their interactions with each other seemed at first pretty brutal—lots of punching and slapping, loud and harsh words screamed at each other. I learned, though, that most of that behavior was all in fun and didn't mean they were actually mad at each other. They'd hug and cheer and charge out onto the field, charged up and ready to give their best. I thought that was pretty cool, and I wanted to be just like those guys."

Matt's dad, Coach John Lawson, was old-school. Concussions were just another part of the game, sometimes even badges of courage. Trainers on the sidelines determined if an injured player seemed okay, meaning he could still stand upright, and then sent him right back into the game. His dad believed, in the words of the famous coach Vince Lombardi, "Winning isn't everything; it's the only thing!"

"And that's how it was at home, too," Matt said to Janet. "When Dad and Mom disagreed, they fought. They never hit each other, but they both yelled at each other and said hurtful things. By sheer force of will, Dad often got his way. But Mom had her own, more subtle ways of holding her own. In either case, it would eventually end like those blustery arguments in the locker room, with hugs and affirming words.

"My brothers and I, though, would get away from the fray as soon as it started and hoped it would end soon. I hated it when it was going on. It could get volatile to the point that I was afraid someone would be mad enough one day to hit the other person, or that my dad would leave us. But that never happened. They're still married, so it obviously worked.

"We can make it work too. Both sides of any issue get told, and the best one wins. We're both relatively smart, and we're both strong—at least strongheaded! We may wrestle a bit until we work it out, and then we kiss and make up! That's my favorite part."

"Sounds kinda scary," Janet replied. "But I get it. As you know, I'm an only child and my parents divorced when I was about six. My mom put herself through school, took care of me, and landed a job with a large corporation. She worked hard to make it into the rarified air of corporate management. So, while I didn't witness fights in my own home, I heard all about her fighting for herself in the workplace. She never backed down when she felt wronged or when she was challenged to prove herself. Sometimes at home she'd cry a little and seem down for a while. But she always bounced back. She's my hero. A woman with a will to win!

"I do the same thing as my mom," Janet continued. "That 'I can do this' attitude shows up the most for me in sports. I'm so competitive and just love spiking that volleyball with an unreturnable blast. When I blow it, my blood just boils until I get into my rhythm again."

More talks like these followed over the remaining college years, and little fights stayed little, adding to the belief that being strong and winning an argument was worth the sporadic discomfort of having to admit defeat. And in the end, they always got to kiss and make up!

Things changed, though, after Matt and Janet got married. The football and the volleyball were on a shelf in the garage, and the arguments took on more weight than winning games or being the one to choose where they went for dinner. Little fights became bigger and bigger. Voices were raised and stinging comments thrown about. And now, their two children were witnessing damaging patterns used for allegedly reconciling differences.

Matt and Janet's relationship was subject to many of the pressures present in marriages today: both partners working demanding jobs, growing children, unexpected expenses, keeping up appearances of success, social networking, and the physical implications of living with no margins. Added to all of these pressures, Matt and Janet had the additional strain of mounting unresolved issues. So far, they had preserved the image of successfully managing all these pressures with the skill of strong, accomplished people.

But internal troubles were simmering inside each of them. Every issue ended with one spouse getting his or her way. That meant the other added more and more hurt and resentment to his or her growing pile of losses. And even when they compromised, it just felt like another name for losing.

One particular argument, though, finally shattered any illusion that fighting was a viable choice in settling disagreements.

"Whose car is in the garage?" Janet asked as she came home from work. She expected to see one or both of their children but not Matt. His car was nowhere in sight, so she assumed he wasn't home yet.

"Hi!" he enthusiastically said as he gave her a big hug.

"Hi?" she said in a questioning voice. "So who's here and why is their car in the garage?"

Before Matt could answer, Janet pushed away from him and said, "You didn't!"

"Now don't blow up," Matt said, with his hands raised in a cautionary way. "I got a great deal and a good trade-in on my old car." He knew what was coming and squared off for a fight.

"We decided *not* to get a new car now! We settled it! You agreed!"

Matt's combative reaction kicked in, and Janet's rage over being ignored burst out. Voices escalated and venomous remarks landed on their intended targets. Matt grabbed Janet on her upper arms, squeezing hard and spewing out threats so close to her face that spit landed on her cheeks. She clawed at his face and screamed for him to let her go.

"Stop it!" yelled their daughter. *"Stop!"*

At first, they didn't even hear their teenage daughter, who stood in the kitchen doorway. She screamed for them to stop again and jumped on her father's back. Matt immediately let go of Janet and knelt by his daughter, now crumpled on the floor. Janet fell down on the other side of their daughter, and all three of them sobbed.

After this terrible fight, Matt and Janet sought help. With a little assistance, they made a truce to stop fighting and stop denying the damage it was doing to them and to their daughters. They finally saw the lie they had bought into and began to find their way out.

Depending on their unique relational style, combative couples often wind up in one of three kinds of dysfunctional relationships:

High-Conflict Relationships

Fights are a regular feature of married life for these couples. The consequences are grim: a growing tally of emotional wounds and bruises; the erosion of feelings that the relationship is safe and secure; and feelings of fear and dread about undergoing more combative conflicts.

Pursue/Withdraw Relationships

In these cases, the pursuing spouse wants to engage in more fights to "work it out" and feels frustrated and shut out when battles don't happen. Meanwhile, the withdrawing spouse feels pursued, threatened, or even trapped.

Withdraw/Withdraw Relationships
When both spouses are more conflict avoidant, or after too many destructive fights, both partners back away from each other and from conflict, seeking relief from pain through disconnection and distancing. This battle is more of a quiet "cold war."

Self-Assessment: How Does Your Team Function?
It's time for a team checkup. Answer the following questions to see how your marriage team functions. The goal here is to do a brief self-evaluation, not to criticize yourself or your spouse. Here is a chance to get to know yourself and your spouse better and to identify where new opportunities exist.

1. How did your parents (or parent and step-parent) handle conflict? What was their unique relational style?

    • High-Conflict Relationship
    • Pursue/Withdraw Relationship
    • Withdraw/Withdraw Relationship

     What impact did the way they handled conflict have on you growing up? How did it influence the way you handle conflict in your marriage?

2. How has Vince Lombardi's mind-set of "Winning isn't everything; it's the only thing!" impacted your marriage relationship? What is the relationship cost of trying to "win" arguments in your marriage?

3. On a scale of 1 to 10, mark the degree to which you agree or disagree with the following statements:

   • In a marriage, a "win-win" is always better than a "win-lose" solution.

   • Because everyone is different and unique, conflict is natural and unavoidable.

   • Men and women need to fight for what they believe in and want in their marriage.

   • It's better for us to fight about important issues than avoid them altogether.

   • Since fighting is natural, and we love each other, we need to remember to "fight fair."

   • Because fights produce winners and losers, marriage means each of us will win some, and each of us will lose some. Such compromises are a necessary part of married life.

   • Since fights cause emotional distance, we must always make up afterward, or we'll just grow apart.

4. How would you define "fair fighting"? What are some of the rules you use in your marriage to fight fair? Explain.

5. What typically happens when you and your spouse try to make a decision?

    • I usually get my way.
    • My spouse usually gets his or her way.
    • We find a compromise.
    • We find a solution that both of us feel good about.

Matt and Janet: Living the Lie

Matt and Janet have embraced a series of basic ideas about love and marriage. We totally love one of their ideas, but the others are dangerous lies that are destroying their marriage.

First, they've grabbed on to one idea that makes perfect sense: Because everyone is different and unique, conflict is natural and unavoidable. We agree 100 percent. This truth is self-evident and is confirmed by our daily experience in the world.

But we worry about some of their other ideas about conflict resolution:

    • Because conflict is natural, men and women need to fight for what they believe in and want in their marriage.

- Since fighting is natural, and we love each other, we need to remember to "fight fair."

- Because fights produce winners and losers, marriage means each of us will win some, and each of us will lose some. Such compromises are a necessary part of married life because, as the Rolling Stones told us decades ago, you can't always get what you want.

- It's better for us to fight about important issues than avoid them altogether.

- And because fights can cause emotional distance, we must always make up afterward, or we'll just grow apart.

We realize many of these ideas seem completely reasonable, but we'll show the problems with them in a moment. But where do people like Matt and Janet get ideas like these? As we've demonstrated throughout this book, we're being taught this stuff every time we turn around. One place is pop culture, which has been serenading people with songs about fighting and making up for decades.

Sixties teen idol Bobby Vinton sounded apologetic in "Let's Kiss and Make Up."

Mary J. Blige revisited the topic in 2014's "Kiss and Make Up": "We argue, but it won't break us."[1]

Katy Perry's 2008 song "Hot N Cold" expresses similar sentiments: "We fight, we break up. We kiss, we make up."[2]

Movies often portray a darker version of intimate combat, none darker than the 1989 film *The War of the Roses*. Michael Douglas and Kathleen Turner play Oliver and Barbara Rose, who meet at a Nantucket auction, fall in love, have two children, and grow fabulously wealthy. But major fault lines appear in the foundation of their marriage, and with the help of battling attorneys, Oliver and Barbara duke it out over ownership of their massive mansion.

The film ends with one final knock-down, drag-out fight. Both Oliver and Barbara claim possession of a huge chandelier, but as they battle over this symbolic possession, the chandelier crashes to the floor. Oliver and Barbara fall with it, dying together amid pieces of broken metal and shards of glass. And while Oliver and Barbara Rose's battles may seem overly dramatic, fights between men and women *can* be deadly: "Over half of the killings of American women are related to intimate partner violence," reported *The Atlantic* in a 2017 article.[3] Also, a 2005 study from the US Department of Justice said that family members committed 3.5 million violent crimes against other family members between 1998 and 2002, with 49 percent of these crimes committed against spouses, typically injuring female partners.[4]

Matt and Janet certainly haven't gone that far, but they've experienced their share of pitched battles and reluctant compromises. They're hurting, and they want to stop hurting each other. Fighting hurts, even when opponents try to fight fair. And the more fights two people engage in, the further apart they can grow. That's why we work with couples to find a better way.

Embracing the Truth

Everyone agrees: Men and women often disagree!

It's a fact. Conflict in marriage is natural and unavoidable. We are different, and our differences will bump against each other. But that's not the end of the story. In reality, conflict is one of the Enemy's favorite playgrounds to mess with couples, and fighting is his tool. Here's why.

The moment you and your spouse square off as adversaries, you're sunk. The only real adversary of your marriage is Satan himself. He wants you dead, and he wants your marriage and family destroyed. But if he can get you to take your eyes off of him, the true adversary, and instead view your spouse as the enemy, he's got you! You've played right into his hands.

You see, by design God created marriage in essence as a team sport. Thus, it operates by the same rules as any team. You either win as a team, or you lose as a team. In reality, there is no such thing as a win-lose outcome in marriage—ever! It's purely an illusion from the pit of hell. That's why Scripture so clearly states, "If a house is divided against itself, that house will not be able to stand" (Mark 3:25).

So infighting on the team only destroys the team and keeps it from being successful. It pits teammates against each other when they're supposed to be pulling together toward a common goal. That's why we've totally rejected the idea of fair fighting. Fighting is fighting, fair or not. Fighting occurs between opponents. When teammates fight, in that moment, they become adversaries.

The lie we've believed in marriage is that sometimes one wins while the other loses, and it all averages out over time. The truth is that if either one loses, both lose! You win together or you lose together. Satan doesn't want us to realize this, because once we see this simple truth, remember it, and operate accordingly, he loses us.

You can't avoid conflict, but you must avoid fighting if you want your marriage to survive and thrive. Fighting *is* avoidable, and we recommend avoiding it whenever you can. It's a horrible way of settling conflicts that can leave deep, lasting scars and hurts, and it assures that you never really win.

But once couples find a healthy way to address marriage conflicts as teammates and friends, these episodes can actually help their love and intimacy grow. People need a marriage where they make love, not war. That's why research Greg did for Focus on the Family exploring what makes a good marriage found that healthy conflict management was an essential trait of thriving marriages.

For couples like Janet and Mark, who experience continual combustible combat, we urge them to move beyond fighting and find a better way to address conflicts. That demands nothing less than a paradigm shift that embraces these three essential truths:

1. Conflict is real because differences between partners are real (and good). These differences are important and cannot be overlooked or swept under the carpet. God makes each and every one of us unique, and then our varied family upbringings and life experiences teach us different lessons about what's important.

When couples fight, these differences are often at the root of the conflict. But fighting about personal differences seldom helps and often hurts. That's because God created each one of you on purpose, and your differences are important to Him, and they are meant to be of use and value to your team.

All great teams are comprised of teammates with various strengths and weaknesses. But, as with all human beings, they don't have the exact same strengths and weaknesses. Those differences allow them to thrive in certain roles better than others. Championship teams learn how to play to each other's strengths and cover each other's weaknesses, enabling them to get the most out of everyone and succeed as a team.

The very same is true of your marriage. Remember when you found your partner's differences attractive and intriguing? Underlying that attractive intrigue is the often-unseen value of a different perspective, skills, and aptitudes you don't personally possess; awareness and sensitivities you don't have but may need; different experiences and knowledge; and plenty more. All you notice at first is the fascinating uniqueness. Smart teammates, though, are constantly on the lookout for how to fully capitalize on the God-given gifts of those they play with.

2. Good marriage partners aren't combatants. They are members of the same team and must work together as one. Once the team players are assembled, they need to work well together. There will be a common goal they are united together to accomplish. When they're clear about the goal and apply themselves in the same direction, they can achieve amazing things. Remember, as we discussed in an earlier chapter, unity is at the heart of oneness. However, when working at odds with each other, little gets done, and we tend to go in circles.

3. Conflicting issues need to be addressed, but not through fighting. We are in no way advocating avoiding the real issues that naturally occur in marriage. They need to be skillfully addressed and managed.

Instead, we are encouraging you to make your marriage a no-fight zone. This merely means that combat as adversaries will not be an acceptable method used to deal with problems and challenges. As lovers and friends, we commit to operating with love and respect, even when the issues push our buttons and trigger our fears.

We want our team to succeed, and we now clearly know that if either walks away from any interaction feeling as if he or she lost, that means that the team—everyone—lost. Therefore, with full recognition of our status as teammates, we will commit to protect each other and the team by adopting a "no losers" policy. Simply stated, that means that we will not settle for either person walking away feeling bad about the way things ended and what we came up with.

The Seven Steps to a Win-Win

You can spend your married life fighting or compromising, but why should you when there's a much better alternative? We challenge you to aim higher: Seek solutions that you both *feel* really good about. That's what we mean by win-win. By the way, this is the communication method we referred to as Work Talk in the last chapter. Greg will walk you through the Seven Steps to a Win-Win and then illustrate them by showing an example of how this tool worked for him and Erin.

"Your mother warned me about this before we got married." These are not the words you want to hear from your wife during an argument, especially after nearly twenty-three years of marriage!

Apparently, as a young boy, I was notorious for engaging my parents in long, arduous debates. I wasn't trying to be disrespectful, but when something didn't make sense to me, when I didn't agree with them or I felt that they were wrong, I would calmly engage my poor parents in lengthy discussions. I learned from a young age that I could win one of these marathon exchanges by simply wearing them down. Eventually, my parents would simply give in or give up out of sheer exhaustion. I was a little hellion in this way!

Unfortunately for Erin, I brought this style of relating straight into my marriage. I'm sure Erin and my parents bonded over this during the early years of our union—misery loves company!

I'd like to think that as I've aged and matured, these types of interactions have lessened; however, a while back I found myself smack in the middle of one of these arduous debates with Erin.

One late Sunday evening, Erin found Garrison, our then-fourteen-year-old son, and me engrossed in a Sunday night NFL game down in our basement—the man cave! It was an epic battle between two elite teams that had come down to the final few minutes.

"You're still watching football?" Erin asked Garrison, sounding surprised. "I thought you had English homework that's due tomorrow."

"I'll get it done," Garrison defended. "The game is almost finished."

"It's almost ten!" Erin countered. "Get upstairs right now and do your homework!"

"But Mom," Garrison begged, "there's only three minutes left and the game is tied. Just let me finish and then I'll get my homework done."

"N . . . O . . . " Erin slowly sounded out her final response to Garrison. "Get to your room N . . . O . . . W!" Defeated, Garrison stomped up the stairs in protest.

"You're being a little rough on the boy," I nonchalantly commented. "There were only a few minutes left."

And that was the exact moment that the power struggle went from Erin versus Garrison to Erin versus Greg.

"What did you just say?" Erin asked, slowly turning her head toward me.

Oh boy, I thought.

"Your son is obsessed with football," Erin argued. "The entire weekend, all he does is watch college football and NFL football. He's an addict!"

Needless to say, the accusation triggered my emotional buttons, and we ended up in one of those grinding two-hour deliberations that I used to have with my parents. I felt that Erin was being unfair to characterize Garrison as *obsessed* or *addicted* for watching football. Really, Erin was just trying to explain that she felt this area of his life was out of balance.

As we argued about Garrison's football-watching habits, it's not that we yelled at each other or said hurtful things. I just exhausted Erin from the mental sparring, and she eventually gave up. Sadly, I won out of attrition—I simply wore her down.

Erin started to climb the stairs to our bedroom. She took a few steps and looked back at me and said, "Your mother warned me about this before we got married."

And that was the end of our "discussion."

The next day, after a relatively sleepless night, we both apologized and worked out a plan around weekend football for our son that we both felt good about. Here is how we found a win-win solution.

Step 1. Adopt the "No Losers" Policy

Even though you may in principle have fully bought into the idea that you either both win or both lose, it's worth reiterating to your spouse that in this moment you are operating with a commitment to both winning. As Erin and I started to talk, I wanted to reiterate that we were on the same team: "Before we begin trying to sort this out, I want to make sure you know that I won't accept any solution here until we both feel really good about it. I want our team to win, and therefore, how you feel is going to matter every bit as much as how I feel." Although leery of my propensity to engage her in another long debate, Erin nodded her head in agreement.

Step 2. Heart Talk the Issue

Since we've defined a win-win as a solution you both *feel* good about, it's hard to arrive at that unless you take the time to find out how each person feels. In the previous chapter we told you that Heart Talk is not meant to be used to solve problems but is designed as a tool for understanding and connecting. When used in its purest form, that's true. However, in the context of problem-solving, it can pull double duty.

In this use of Heart Talk, you still want to care about the feelings of your spouse, but you are also mining critical information.

If I want to find a solution we both love, I need to clearly know how I feel so I can make sure it's accounted for. But it's every bit as important to really know how Erin feels. In this case, the more of the emotional data I have, the easier it is to creatively find options we can both like. Without it, it's more like shooting in the dark and hoping you hit something.

"What was going on for you last night?" I asked Erin.

"Your comment that I was being 'rough' on Garrison left me feeling like the villain—the mean old mom trying to wreck everyone's fun. Garrison is really struggling in English, and his grade is slipping. If it goes too low, he won't be able to play basketball for his school. I felt unsupported and alone—that it's solely my job to worry about his grades."

I tried to mirror back what I was hearing Erin express. "So you didn't feel supported by me and feel Garrison's grades are solely your responsibility."

"Yes, absolutely. What about you?" Erin asked. "What was going on for you last night?"

"My mom used to do the same thing to me when I was a teenager," I explained. "She would get frustrated with my dad and would kick me out of the living room, where we had the only TV. I always felt disrespected when she did that to me. Last night, Garrison and I had invested several hours into that game. So when you made him leave with only a few minutes left, I felt cheated out of enjoying the final outcome with my son, and I felt disrespected—like my decision to let him watch the game was wrong in your eyes. Instead of talking about it, you just kicked him out."

"So you felt cheated that you didn't get to finish the game together and disrespected because I told him to leave without checking with you first."

"Yes," I affirmed Erin, "you listened perfectly."

Step 3. Pray for Unity

This powerful step serves two important purposes. First, we don't ever want to try to overcome our challenges without the benefit of the Lord's wisdom and guidance. I took Erin's hand and we prayed, "Lord, we are not together on this. We are not on the same page. But we truly desire unity. Please help us find a solution we both feel good about. Thank You for being in the middle of this with us."

But the wonderful added benefit here is that as soon as you pray *together* for God's help, you've already restored unity, even prior to finding a win-win solution. Notice, you were not together before this: my ideas versus your ideas, my feelings versus your feelings. However, now you join together and ask God to help you find a solution you both feel great about. From this point forward the two of you are working together with God—unity is restored. All you need now is a solution.

Step 4. Brainstorm Your Options

This is the work step. Use any methods you can think of to find ideas and possibilities you both might feel good about. Talk to people who've dealt with similar issues, google it, get creative. Most commonly, just get out a piece of paper and start writing down each other's ideas. Don't be afraid to suggest "crazy" ideas. If they are truly crazy, you can throw them out later. But often, it's some of the craziest ideas that lead to options that turn out to be brilliant. (*You know, that was crazy, but it got me to thinking about X.*)

If you have an idea rattling around in your head, get it out by writing it down.

"What is it that you need from me to feel supported around Garrison's grades?" I asked.

"I don't want to be the only one asking if his homework is

completed or if he's studied for an upcoming test," Erin responded. "I want us to be a team around his English grade."

"Absolutely," I agreed. "I want us both to help him succeed in school."

"What do you need from me?" Erin asked.

"I want to feel included in how we hold him accountable," I explained.

"Sounds good to me," Erin responded.

Step 5. Evaluate Options and Choose One You Both Feel Good About

This step is fairly self-explanatory. Just remember you're not looking to settle or compromise but to hang in there until both of you feel as if you've landed on a win-win.

As Erin and I sat there, suddenly an idea hit me. "What if Garrison picks the one football game that he really wants to watch, and then we make a new rule that he can't watch it until his homework is done. We can always record the game if he needs extra time or help with his homework or preparing for a test."

"I love that idea," Erin replied. "And then we can do some other things as a family besides watching football."

Step 6. Try It

This step is essential. Just because it *sounded* like a win-win when you were talking about it doesn't mean it will feel like one when you try it.

Step 7. Check Back In and Rework It, If Necessary

This process is actually another feedback loop, just like the Care Cycle. So after trying the idea out, make sure you both feel good about how it's going. If this solution is not working out for both of you, cycle back up and reassert your commitment to the "no losers" policy. Heart Talk what felt good and what didn't. Pray for additional help. Brainstorm new options or tweaks to what you already had. Come with the new win-win, try it, and reevaluate. Don't quit until you're both pleased with the result.

After implementing the new rule with Garrison, his grade in English improved. The hardest part of our win-win plan was the fact that there are college football games all day Saturday and NFL games all day Sunday, Monday night, and now Thursday night— it's like the NFL is trying to take over the world! The US could be invaded by some foreign enemy and no one would even notice because we're all watching football! So we have to keep tweaking the plan so Garrison and I can watch a few other great games while maintaining balance.

One of the things that make this so powerful for believers is that we serve a God who is committed to unity. He lives in a perfectly unified triune relationship: Father, Son, and Holy Spirit. He wants nothing more than to also be in unity with us and to help us be in unity with each other. It does require a little faith to test this out, but this seven-step process gives us a golden opportunity to watch the Lord demonstrate His commitment to us over and over again. It has been a huge faith builder for us and countless others who've had the courage to try. We hope and pray for your encouragement and success too!

Win-Win Exercises

Adopt Your Own "No Losers" Policy

Remember, in a marriage, you are on the same team. Thus, you either win together or lose together. There is no such thing as a win-lose because you're on the same team. As you work toward finding win-win solutions in your marriage, put into practice Philippians 2:4: "Let each of you look not only to your own interests, but also to the interests of others." Start with writing your own "no losers" policy. Make it unacceptable for either person to walk away feeling as if he or she lost. Redefine winning as finding a solution that feels good to both people. For example, "We will no longer accept any solution until we both feel really good about it. We want our team to win, and therefore, how you feel is going to matter every bit as much as how I feel."

As you articulate your own "no losers" policy, you instantly create safety. When people aren't worried about protecting their own agenda, defending their position, getting walked over, or being taken advantage of, they relax. When you are no longer anxious that your feelings and ideas won't be considered, the worry disappears and is replaced by hope. When you believe that your spouse also wants what is best for you, your heart opens, and this paves the way for creativity. And a win-win solution is best found when the creative juices are flowing.

Try a Win-Win Practice Round

You can practice finding win-win solutions on any issues you'd like to discuss. For couples like Matt and Janet, we urge them to start with smaller issues until they get the hang of functioning as a team under a "no losers" policy.

Pick a fun topic like your ideal date night. Take turns describing in detail the perfect date together. Would it be a day date or evening together? Would it be over a few hours or would you spend the night somewhere? Where would you eat? What would you do (dinner and a movie, hiking, attending a sporting event, concert, or Broadway show, coffee, something else)? How would you end your date? Practice your Heart Talk skills—listening and repeating back what you hear your spouse saying. Now create a win-win date night by taking elements from both date nights and combining them into one perfect date. Finally, put this date on the calendar—and enjoy!

CONCLUSION:

PUTTING IT ALL TOGETHER

Throughout this book you've explored nine of the most common lies we encounter in our work with couples. These falsehoods influence how most of us think about and approach our marriage relationships. Generally, none of us even realize that these ideas have set us up for frustration and disappointment—and possibly, even complete failure.

These notions are usually passed on to us by well-meaning people who really believe they are the keys to marital bliss. Rarely have our encouragers wanted anything other than to help us. Both of us, Greg and Bob, believed and attempted to use most of them only later to discover how so many of our relational hurts and disappointments could trace their origins back to one or more of these misguided strategies.

These relationship beliefs and strategies have infiltrated our culture, and many have even become prominent within the church. That's why we've presented these common misunderstandings and unfortunate approaches—so you can consider if they've also been responsible for some of your own frustrations and disappointments. Have some of these ideas contributed to your inability to capture all that your hearts have longed for with your spouse and in your marriage?

Rooting out the lies is important, but perhaps you've also noticed the ideas and tools in this book that can turn the course of your relationship around. When skillfully used, they have the power to set you on a new course toward personal and marital success and satisfaction.

In fact, over the years we've discovered that much of what we uncovered in our "marriage lab" actually fits together in a wonderfully logical and usable pattern. Not surprisingly, the Healthy Marriage Model diagram below provides a picture of the ideal marital framework, and we believe it reflects a beautiful and elegantly simple depiction of God's preferred design for marriage. All of the tools we have shared here can be understood within this diagram and structure.

HEALTHY MARRIAGE MODEL

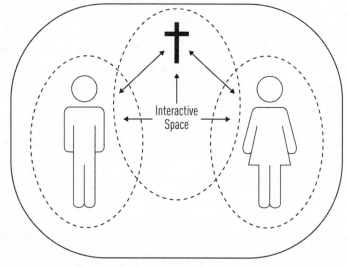

Interactive Space

What we'd like to do now is present a summary of the primary pieces of this puzzle, showing again where they all fit and how the parts function together. And then we'll provide some tips on how to best use them. Remember, our goal continues to be helping you and your team (marriage, or marriage and family) be phenomenally effective and successful.

Our hope is that you will each be personally successful and fulfilled, while operating in the center of your design and calling. Additionally, we pray that your children and all near you will revel with you in the relationship you've created and enjoy. And finally, we pray that you and everyone you encounter will be inspired by the picture of what you are proving is possible for all who walk in Christ and live according to His design for His children. In the end, your marriage creates a legacy that has genuine Kingdom impact and carries on for generations!

Ryan and Ashley

Remember our friends Ryan and Ashley? We'd like to use a little more of their story to help us demonstrate the model in action. They, like each of us, are normal, imperfect people trying to find their way through all the noise and craziness. They each grew up in normal, less than perfect families, subject to the same cultural teachings, and surrounded by well-meaning people wanting to help them succeed.

They each brought their own relational and emotional baggage to the marriage, and their hearts were impacted by this fallen world long before they ever met. But in spite of all that, they both shared a desire for a great marriage filled with love and mutual fulfillment and satisfaction.

You may remember that they dodged a bullet at their wedding ceremony when someone helped them steer clear of the unity candle imagery. But we saw later that they did get a full dose of the "you need to meet each other's needs" idea. With that codependent belief firmly in place—and even encouraged by the pastor—they set out together with great hopes of realizing all of their marital dreams.

Unfortunately, like most of us, the relationship they ended up with was far from what their hearts had longed for. Ryan invested himself in faithfully doing everything he could to grow in his career and provide for his family, which frequently left him distracted.

Ashley at first was excited about the journey she had begun with her "Mr. Right," and did everything she could think of to be his "Mrs. Right." But the connection and fulfillment she longed for always stayed just out of reach. As time progressed, that dream seemed to slip even further from her grasp.

Knowing something was wrong, Ashley began to voice her feelings of disappointment and emptiness to Ryan. Yet no matter how Ryan responded, the situation only seemed to get worse. So Ashley proceeded to complain more often and with increased intensity, feebly praying it might make a difference. At some point Ryan grew so exasperated by what felt like futility, he eventually threw up his hands in defeat.

That's how they ended up in one of our intensives. Ashley's mom had discovered that there was trouble in paradise and heard about Focus on the Family's Hope Restored Intensives on a Focus radio broadcast. She gave the contact information to Ashley, who brought it to Ryan. They prayed about it, knowing they desperately needed help. Ultimately, they felt led to attend the intensive.

Reactive Cycle

Early in their intensive they were introduced to the Reactive Cycle. For the first time they each were able to clearly see why their conflict continued to spin miserably no matter what they tried. They saw how each had buttons from their past that they brought with them to the marriage. Ashley did not cause Ryan's fears of failure. Ryan began developing that sensitivity long before they met. But when Ashley voiced her frustration and disappointment in Ryan and their marriage, she sure did push that button!

In the same way, Ryan did not create Ashley's fear of not measuring up. But when, in Ashley's eyes, he seemed more committed to work and other things away from her, he stomped all over that button!

By studying their personal Reactive Cycle hanging on the wall in front of them, they were each able to see some of the ways they were unfairly placing blame on the other. They also saw how incredibly disempowering and useless that blame was.

So let's see where the parts of Ryan and Ashley's relationship described above live and operate within our model.

REACTIVE CYCLE

Ryan and Ashley had experienced hurts and disappointments in their lives. Buttons, fears, beliefs, and expectations are all born through our life experiences, our interpretations of those experiences, and much of what we are taught along the way. As you look at the model, notice that all of those items exist within the individual.

However, when any two people interact, especially when our hearts are engaged, our fears, beliefs, and expectations frequently bump into each other in troubling ways. The resulting unpleasant feelings commonly propel us to react as an attempt to eliminate, reduce, or change those emotions. But as we react as a way to make ourselves feel better, we frequently push the buttons of the person we're interacting with. As a result, that person now reacts, which then pushes another button of the first person, and we're off to the Reactive Cycle races!

The first big realization both Ryan and Ashley had at the intensive was merely the fact that this predictable cycle was constantly at play underneath their conflicts. Sadly, this cycle had now become their most common interactive pattern.

For them to now see the pure futility of this craziness was helpful, but they initially had no idea how to stop the madness. When they learned that they each had the power to stop the cycle by simply creating space between their personal buttons and reactions, they were relieved and empowered. Instead of unconsciously reacting, they could resist the emotional pull and instead choose to not react—regardless of what the other did. The first time Ryan tried it, he was amazed at how powerful self-control actually felt, as he skillfully sidestepped an almost-certain Reactive Cycle!

But as useful as this new insight and skill was, now what? Simply not reacting to each other certainly didn't make for a better life and marriage. Fortunately, stopping the Reactive Cycle is not the end: It's just the beginning of creating the marriage of their dreams.

Safe and Secure

Ryan and Ashley were now fully awakened to the frequency of their previously unconscious cycle of conflict and had learned how to stop it. But they realized they wanted more than simply to stop reacting. The intensive therapist had just spent a few minutes talking about the foundational importance of feeling safe and secure. They each were captivated by a new vision for what their relationship could be. How they had been relating to each other had created an increasingly unsafe and insecure environment. Together they committed to change that.

The two of them actually became excited about the prospect of finally living together in a way that felt incredibly safe and secure. How different would that be? Just the thought of it caused their shoulders to relax and a sigh of relief to escape their lips. They wanted to feel safe and secure enough to be comfortable just being who they were created to be and to no longer have to feel so on guard with each other.

So they began by reassuring each other that they were fully committed. Ryan leaned slightly forward and looked directly into Ashley's eyes and said, "Honey, I want you to know I still love you deeply, with my whole heart. I am so grateful for our friendship, and you are the one I want to walk with through life. Right now I want to restate what my intention was on the day I married you: I commit to love in good times and in bad, till death do us part. I will never leave you nor forsake you!"

A warm smile appeared on Ashley's lips, and a gentle tear ran down her cheek. She felt oddly caught off guard by the seriousness of the moment and decided to lighten the mood a bit. With a playful grin she looked at Ryan and said, "Back at ya, big boy!" Then she winked and blew Ryan a kiss. They both grinned at each other, and Ryan took Ashley's hand and gave it a light squeeze.

Over the next few minutes they each put in words a personal commitment to work toward becoming an increasingly trustworthy person for the other. Ashley described how much she wanted to really pay attention to Ryan's feelings in ways she now saw she had never done before. Hearing Ashley make his feelings and experience that important felt surprisingly good to Ryan. He thanked her for caring about him like that.

The picture of what they were setting out to create together was becoming clearer and clearer. Ryan then said, "You know, I really want us to enjoy being truly relaxed and secure together. I know I can get good at this. In fact, I not only intend to respect and care for your heart, I want to make it safe for all of you: body, mind, and spirit, too!"

He continued by adding, "And if I really want us to feel safe and secure together, I see that I absolutely have to become a man I can trust. I want us both to enjoy the best of me. Therefore, Ashley, I'm committing to learn how to skillfully and consistently care well for myself. If I'm empty, or even half-empty, neither of us are getting my best. With God's help, that's gonna change."

They both acknowledged that if all they had just discussed was consistently attended to by both of them, the foundation of their marriage would be solid. Together they were setting out to create the ideal relational environment for an intimate connection to thrive. Again, they both looked at each other and smiled.

Care Cycle

Returning to their Reactive Cycle chart, they were next shown that when either had a button pushed and they found enough self-control to not react, they could then emotionally step back, focus inward, and use the Care Cycle. Stopping the Reactive Cycle is great and is certainly better than spinning. But creating space alone does not move the person or the marriage forward. However, the Care Cycle does.

This tool enables each of them to first figure out what's going on within themselves, what they could personally do to feel attended to and cared for, and then to take the steps necessary to assure they actually get cared for.

CARE CYCLE

For example, Ashley was excited to now have options she could use to get to a better place, without being so powerless and dependent on Ryan. She was sick of feeling frustrated and angry all the time! In the past, any time Ryan pulled back, regardless of why he did, she felt abandoned. She hated the woman she became when those feelings took over and wanted to get back to being the kind, caring, devoted wife and friend she knew she actually was created to be.

The Care Cycle provided a way to assure she could succeed. She knew her old codependent habits would be hard to break and that learning to care well for herself would take time. But she was sure with practice and a little patience, she could master it.

Ryan was overjoyed by Ashley's new insights and was sure using the Care Cycle would really bless her. But personally, he saw that his deeply ingrained caretaker mind-set left him frequently ignored and also unattended to. Ryan could clearly see how taking the time to care well for himself would actually enable him to have even more to give to Ashley and others. By making sure he stayed full, whole, and healthy, he would be better for everyone—himself included!

He knew that at times caring for himself would also require setting loving boundaries. He now saw Ashley in a whole new way, as a fully empowered and beautiful *adult* woman, capable of caring well for her own heart. He wanted a close and connected relationship with Ashley and was committed to loving her well. He didn't want the job of "taking care of her." He saw that seeing her as someone needing to be taken care of actually subtly led to treating her as if she were an emotional child. That wasn't good for either of them.

In the past, when Ashley's codependency would rise up, or she had any doubts about herself and her ability to get herself to a better place, she normally looked to Ryan to make it better. His codependent "caretaker" side would kick in, and in the end neither liked the way their relationship worked.

Instead, Ryan was now learning to responsibly take care of Ryan while standing solidly right by her side. He didn't have to choose to care for one over the other. He could encourage *Ashley* to take good care of *Ashley*. He could be a great lover and friend, be a source of assistance and support, without feeling responsible *for* her. In time he knew he could learn to resist the codependent pull and care well for both of them with gentleness and grace.

The light bulb had really gone off for both Ryan and Ashley. The Care Cycle provided a key missing ingredient in their marriage. They were excited about what the other tools would provide, but they both knew that the Care Cycle alone would finally free their relationship to achieve more of what they both were longing for.

Heart Talk

Now, from a centered and personally empowered place of feeling well attended to and cared for, either Ryan or Ashley may decide there's something they've learned worth sharing with the other.

This could include feelings they believe would be valuable for their spouse to know about, or feelings they sense their spouse is having that they'd like to understand and care about. In either case, Heart Talk is an ideal tool to use for a good heart-to-heart talk. Engaging in emotional communication is a powerful move toward intimacy with each other, and it's an essential step in building a satisfying and fulfilling close and connected marriage.

From the inwardly focused place of employing the Care Cycle, the step of using Heart Talk involves turning your eyes back toward your spouse and the relationship. Functionally it is a step into the center relational circle. Once there, you can invite your spouse to join you for a possible moment of friendship. As you share this time and space together, you deepen your relationship by getting to know each other in new and fresh ways.

HEART TALK

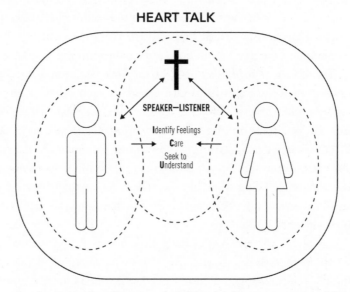

At the intensive, Ryan and Ashley had some amazing Heart Talks. They were so grateful for a safe and secure way to open up and share some of their more vulnerable feelings. It was so refreshing to have their hearts heard, cared for, and validated. Ryan was thrilled that he could care well for Ashley's feelings even when he felt differently. With Heart Talk, Ashley could finally see a way to be able to share what was on her heart while at the same time caring about Ryan's feelings, without the pressure for either to choose one's feelings over the other.

This tool proved so valuable they were determined to get good at it. They knew practice was essential. Together they committed to spend a minimum of five minutes per day practicing Heart Talk even with little things, just to get used to it.

As the weeks passed, this way of communicating increasingly became a more comfortable and familiar way for the couple to talk together anytime emotions were involved. They especially noticed that, at times when buttons got pushed, it was nice to feel confident and skilled as opposed to their old feelings of dread and danger. This tool has already helped them avoid a few buttons that they know in the past would have sent them spinning.

The result of regularly using Heart Talk has been a notable increase in feeling close and connected to each other. They've always wanted to feel safe and comfortable together, more like they did in the beginning of their relationship. These days the love flows freely again. And in those moments when issues arise and buttons bump into each other, they are far less worried about that old wedge being stuck between them. Once their initial raw emotions have settled back down, they each know just what to do to reconnect.

Recently Ryan and Ashley had a little bump. Ashley seemed to get upset when Ryan informed her that he had a big project deadline fast approaching and would need to work late over the next couple of weeks. As if that wasn't bad enough, it included needing to cancel a date to attend a concert they had planned two months earlier. Ryan was both sorry and saddened by this reality, humbly apologized, and promised to make it up to her.

Ashley handled her disappointment with as much grace as she could manage and didn't blow up or get nasty at all. Ryan was impressed but noticed that he was significantly stirred up anyway.

After a little time passed and his emotions settled a bit, Ryan used the Care Cycle to attempt to understand and care about what was going on inside him. With some devoted attention, and a little divine assistance, he stumbled on to a couple of big realizations about himself that he'd never fully seen before.

He set about caring for himself in a new way, which felt much better than his previous style of telling himself to "suck it up and get over it!" He also knew these new insights would be really valuable to share with Ashley.

So he found her reading in the living room. He respectfully interrupted and asked, "Ashley, I see you're reading, but I wondered if I might be able to talk with you for a few minutes? After telling you about my work situation I noticed I was triggered, so I went and used the Care Cycle to sort it out. I ended up with a couple of *aha*s I'd love to share with you, if you're up for a Heart Talk."

Ashley put down her book and said, "Actually, this is a great time. I'd love to hear what's up for you."

So off they went. Ryan began sharing with Ashley his newly rediscovered memories of some childhood interactions with his grandfather. For the first time he was able to connect the dots to how his relationship with his grandfather, and the relationship between his grandfather and grandmother, had contributed to the intensity of his beliefs about how he was supposed to be with his wife and how his wife was supposed to feel as a result. He was also able to see how he transferred those beliefs to his relationship with Ashley.

Without sharing all the details here, the conversation was meaningful for both Ryan and Ashley. She was able to appreciate in a new way how Ryan's caretaker role had become so deeply entrenched, and why her husband's feelings became so intense anytime she seemed upset. Ashley really appreciated Ryan letting her into his heart so she could get to know him better. There was no blame, which made the whole conversation easier for everyone.

She was also able to share a bit about why she got a little hurt by him having to cancel their date. They weren't sure there was much they could do about any of it, but they sure were thankful to have a tender heart-to-heart moment of understanding and caring. With all of their feelings expressed, and both feeling cared for and validated, Ashley was able to talk about her lingering disappointment. And rather than just accepting this less than ideal outcome, she wondered out loud if there might be any options available that might allow a way of proceeding that would feel better to both of them.

Work Talk

Now, as we've shown, Heart Talk is the tool to connect heart to heart and get to know each other more deeply and intimately. Sometimes Heart Talk is all you need. But other times something feels unresolved and needs additional attention. Heart Talk is not the right tool for getting things done and resolving conflicts and problems. Work Talk is the right tool for that job.

As you'll remember, Work Talk is where we invoke our "no losers" policy and pursue win-win outcomes. Any time we're deciding a course of action, but especially when we're dealing with an actual conflict, we begin by reminding ourselves that we're teammates, not adversaries. We overtly refuse to be pawns in the game of the real Enemy, who wants us to square off and fight!

Using our tool Seven Steps to a Win-Win is our recommended option.

SEVEN STEPS TO A WIN-WIN

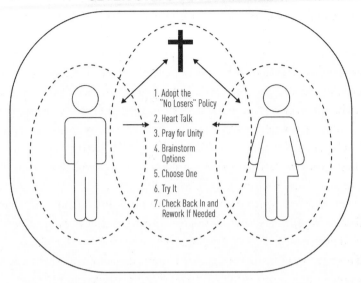

1. Adopt the "No Losers" Policy
2. Heart Talk
3. Pray for Unity
4. Brainstorm Options
5. Choose One
6. Try It
7. Check Back In and Rework If Needed

Ideally, this functions as a simple feedback loop, meaning that we begin knowing we won't settle until the Lord has helped us find a solution we both feel good about. We continue working our way through the steps until we arrive at a mutually acceptable outcome. We may have no idea up front what a win-win would actually look like here, or how we could possibly find such a result given the nature of our differences. But as people of faith who serve a God devoted to unity, we just know somehow the Lord will help us.

With regards to Ryan and Ashley's disappointing date dynamic, they could easily have just accepted that life circumstances simply dealt them a reality they had to manage. Sometimes life goes that way. But in this case, before merely accommodating, they decided to see if there might be options they hadn't yet seen that both of them might like better.

In fact, after taking time to clearly hear each other's hearts, they prayerfully asked God to help them see beyond the obvious, just in case there might be something they had overlooked. They grabbed a pad of paper and listed the circumstances: date planned with tickets purchased, deadline looming, and too little time to work with. They then listed how each felt: feelings about the date and each longing to enjoy time together, the pressure regarding the incomplete project, fears of not meeting the deadline, and more.

Once that was all laid out in front of them, they transitioned to brainstorming possible options. They started with all the more obvious possibilities but then attempted to get creative. Their commitment was to remain unwilling to accept any solution unless both of them felt good about it.

This whole process took about an hour, but in the end, they were both surprised that a series of steps emerged that would enable them to maintain their date without compromising Ryan's ability to get his work done. In this particular case, they uncovered a few other family responsibilities that Ryan was carrying that Ashley was willing to temporarily take over to free some time for Ryan.

In the end, they both felt great about the outcome. But perhaps even more than that, they were so encouraged by the creative and respectful process they went through to find a win-win. In this case the circumstances were fairly lightweight compared to some situations they've dealt with. However, they were excited to think they could learn to use these same steps to manage more difficult and complex situations too.

More even than the potential joy of the date itself, they were operating as an effective team and as friends and lovers. They began to feel as if, with God's help, there was little they could imagine encountering they wouldn't be able to handle together. The fear of having to just "suck it up and settle" was disappearing.

We celebrate with Ryan and Ashley about how differently their marriage is operating and how hopeful they feel. We know we've shared some relatively benign examples. But we also know that these same strategies and tools work with even the most challenging issues. How do we know? We use them ourselves.

Jenni and I (Bob) have transformed our marriage from one where we used to struggle constantly to one we both love. And we love the direction it's heading. We not only love each other deeply, we act as if we do . . . even when our buttons get pushed! It may take a few minutes to gather ourselves and get back on track, but today we typically get there quickly. Relational fear has largely left our marriage.

And I (Greg) have an amazing relationship with Erin. We both have strong feelings about lots of stuff. We bump into periodic conflict because we're fundamentally so different in so many ways. But we deal with our differences as friends and with respect. We refuse to operate as adversaries. We are unwilling to allow the Enemy to have his way with us and our family.

We (Bob and Greg) are so certain that our Lord wants us, as His children, to be unusually successful in our lives and marriages. When managed well, our relationships have the potential not only to bless us but also to be a source of hope and encouragement of what is possible with Christ at the helm. Operating within His design and plan enables us as couples to present the Good News in remarkable ways. Our marriages, then, not only create a beautiful legacy for our families; they create a legacy for the ages! Successful, God-centered marriages help demonstrate what Christians claim is available to all.

Opportunity and Vision

We hope this book has blessed you as an individual, encouraged you as a couple, and equipped you to make your marital dreams come true. And if any of that is true, we feel as if we've succeeded— in part. However, to conclude this book, we'd like to clearly spell out a central underlying motive that helped inspire us to write it.

We certainly do want each of you to have your deepest long-ings for a great marriage and family fulfilled. But at Focus on the Family, we're additionally seeking a far bigger outcome. We exist as a ministry committed to seeing redeemed families, communities, and societies worldwide through Christ. We show up at work every day with Kingdom purposes in mind.

One of the cultural situations we're sadly watching unfold before our eyes is the institution of marriage descending into a troubling state of dishonor. We hear people today commonly question whether marriage as we've historically known it is now being seen as an out-of-date institution. Some ask, "Is traditional marriage between a man and woman even relevant in our world today?" Others ask, "Is marriage even necessary today?" "Aren't two people living together in a committed, loving relationship just as good?" We're sure that with only a little thought you can come up with plenty of your own versions of these cultural shifts.

We are deeply saddened to see continual evidence of societal decline and are convinced that for our culture to thrive and remain healthy, vibrant marriages must be at the center. As Bible-believing Christ followers, we are certain the traditional institution of mar-riage is a cornerstone of God's plan and design for the world. We also believe Hebrews 13:4, which says that marriage should be honored by all.

Therefore, we are tirelessly working with Hebrews 13:4 as our goal—to see marriage restored to its rightful place of honor! We are sure that if we can turn the tide of decline, everyone will benefit. We know we are not alone in our concerns and are unwilling to watch things we care about crumble before our eyes.

So what does any of that have to do with you? Where do you and your marriage fit in?

First and foremost, the fundamental claim of Christianity is that a personal relationship with Christ will make a material difference in your personal life and in your marriage.

You'll notice that our Healthy Marriage Model is founded on the central idea that the health and well-being of the person is critical. Since our Lord is essential for life, personal well-being, and eternal purpose, we're committed to help each person we encounter become full, whole, healthy, and connected to their reason for being. The more we progress toward experiencing the above blessings, the more we prove what we as a body of believers claim to be truth. So that's where we begin.

Then as we encounter a marriage of two people on a journey to become all they were created to be as individuals, we turn our attention to helping them create an over-the-top, awesome marriage. This will always be a relationship of two imperfect people on a journey together, because we're all less than perfect. But this imperfect journey of imperfect people can be meaningful, rich, and enjoyable. Ideally, it will include a clear vision of the bigger purposes of our marriages, beyond just our personal satisfaction. God wants us to use our marriages to bless others. God doesn't want us to hoard His blessings.

He certainly doesn't want "Dead Sea" marriages. The Jordan River is the only major water source flowing into the Dead Sea. However, there are no outlet streams. All of this life-giving water from the Jordan River goes into the Dead Sea, but nothing flows out. God doesn't want Dead Sea marriages. He blesses us so we can bless others. Hebrews 13:16 says, "Do not neglect to do good and to share what you have, for such sacrifices are pleasing to God." Don't neglect to share what you've been given in your marriage, even if it's merely being an encouragement by having a great marriage that proves what is possible with Christ. Remember, true sacrifice is giving away something that we *own* and *value* as an investment in someone else. This is the highest action of love: God doesn't want us to be takers; He wants us to be sacrificial givers, people who invest in others by sharing the many gifts they have been given.

How will you use your marriage to bless others?

We encourage you to develop a shared vision for what you're passionate about pursuing together that will bless other marriages. Zechariah 8:13 says, "So will I save you, and you shall be a blessing." God united you together in oneness in order for you to both experience a remarkable relationship and to do amazing things through it. As much as we pray for great things for you, your marriage should be about something bigger than individual gratification, petty arguments, and the pursuit of pleasure.

Inwardly focused marriages are not deeply fulfilling. That's a Dead Sea marriage. If we only focus on ourselves, our God-given longing to have our lives matter and to make a difference in the world goes unfulfilled. Francis Chan said, "Picture marriage as a vehicle for mission, an opportunity for Christians to carry out our mission to make disciples of all the nations."[1]

Let others be blessed by your marriage, even while you're still imperfect people on an imperfect journey—just as they are. In fact, the details of *what* you pursue together are less important than that you are pursuing something *together*. Being united in vision and pursuing something together (true oneness) is what will most powerfully inspire and bless others. We encourage you to take some time to pray together and ask these questions:

- What kind of marriage legacy do we want to leave?
- In what specific ways are we creating a marriage worth repeating for our children?
- What might God be calling us to do together to serve Him and bless other couples?

Commit to prayer whatever the Lord begins revealing to you and your spouse. We would also love to invite you to join with us and become a champion for marriage. A "marriage champion" is a married individual or couple who work to keep their own marriage strong and invest in other married individuals or couples. Research suggests that if enough of us lock arms around these ideas, we can create a cultural shift and restore marriage to its rightful place of honor.[2] Will you stand with us?

Some additional good news is that investing in other couples can be super simple. Perhaps you want to encourage other married couples by regularly praying for them, celebrating weddings or anniversaries, going on a double date with another couple, or providing childcare for a younger couple. All these actions demonstrate your belief that marriage is important and is something to be honored.

Maybe you'd be willing to take it a step further and meet one-on-one with a same-sex friend or colleague who is struggling in his or her marriage. You can share your own marriage journey, read a book together, search together to find answers to issues, and help give that person hope during a challenging time. Sometimes a marriage can survive off of someone else's hope for a season!

Or perhaps you undertake formal training so you can mentor an engaged couple, lead a marriage Bible study or small group, or work with couples in crisis. However God might be calling you to invest in other marriages, Focus on the Family would love to equip and support you. Visit www.focusonthefamily.com/marriage for more information.

Imagine a church filled with people connected to the Lord, committed to personal health and well-being, and in marriages that supported those individual journeys while on a mission together to help other couples have strong marriages. That's our dream.

We know this dream is possible because that's what we, and

many we know, are living. We are daily involved in doing everything in our power to help others experience the fullness of God's blessings. That includes developing numerous resources and opportunities that support marriage champions as we try to turn our nation's attitude toward marriage to one of honor and value. But we can't do this alone. For us to pull off this audacious goal, we need you!

We need a groundswell of thousands and thousands of marriage champion couples doing the same thing, both aware of and connected with each other. As a body of believers enjoying the blessings of faith, we *become* the Good News for a desperate and hurting world. Will you help us prove to the world what's possible in a Christ-centered marriage? Will you lock arms with us in our efforts to turn the tide of our culture and help move the Kingdom of God forward?

God bless you as you build a marriage that you are thrilled with, and God bless you as you invest in other couples. We look forward to hearing from you. Together, with God's direction and help, we can once again see a nation filled with healthy, thriving marriages and families.

ABOUT THE AUTHORS

Dr. Greg Smalley serves as the vice president of marriage at Focus on the Family and has a doctorate in psychology. Prior to joining Focus, Smalley worked for the Center for Relationship Enrichment at John Brown University and as President of the National Institute of Marriage. He is the author or coauthor of twenty books including *Reconnected: Moving from Roommates to Soulmates in Your Marriage, Crazy Little Thing Called Marriage,* and *Fight Your Way to a Better Marriage* and is the coauthor of *The DNA of Relationships for Couples.* He and his wife, Erin, have been married for more than twenty-eight years.

Dr. Robert S. Paul, a licensed professional counselor, is vice president of the Focus on the Family Marriage Institute. He is the director and creator of the Hope Restored marriage intensive counseling program. Robert received his bachelor's degree from Evangel University, his master's degree from Georgia State University, and a diploma in Christian counseling and an honorary doctorate from Psychological Studies Institute. He has appeared on numerous radio and television programs and has coauthored three books:

The DNA of Relationships, with Drs. Gary and Greg Smalley; *The DNA of Relationships for Couples*, with Dr. Greg Smalley; and *Finding Ever After*. He is a former professor at Evangel University, where he taught in both the biblical studies and psychology departments. Robert and his wife, Jenni, have been married for more than thirty-nine years.

NOTES

LIE #3: ALL YOU NEED IS LOVE

1. Gary Smalley and John Trent, *Love Is a Decision: Proven Techniques to Keep Your Marriage Alive and Lively* (Nashville: Thomas Nelson, 1989), 5.
2. Larry Norman, "Reader's Digest," side 2, track 5 on *Only Visiting This Planet*, AIR Studios, 1972, https://genius.com/larry-norman-readers-digest-lyrics.
3. Erich Fromm, *The Art of Loving* (New York: Perennial, 2006), 52.
4. Fromm, *The Art of Loving*, 99.
5. Smalley and Trent, *Love Is a Decision*, 5.
6. Grant Cardone, "Love Is a Decision," *The Blog, HuffPost Life*, updated November 17, 2011, https://www.huffpost.com/entry/love-is-a-decision_b_166177.

LIE #4: I MUST SACRIFICE WHO I AM FOR THE SAKE OF MY MARRIAGE

1. Jim Gaffigan Show (@gaffiganshow). 2016. "My wife always asks me why I don't make the bed. And I respond with the same reason why I don't tie my shoes after I take them off." Twitter, August 6, 2016, 8:18 a.m. https://twitter.com/gaffiganshow/status/761944490567430145.
2. Kate Bratskeir, "Why You Should Never Make Your Bed," *Healthy Living, HuffPost Life*, September 23, 2015, https://www.huffpost.com/entry/make-your-bed-dust-mites_n_5601809ce4b08820d91a3e8f.

LIE #6: OUR DIFFERENCES ARE IRRECONCILABLE
1. Gary Smalley, *Secrets to Lasting Love: Uncovering the Keys to Life-Long Intimacy* (New York: Simon & Schuster, 2000), 94–95.
2. Max Lucado, *When God Whispers Your Name* (Nashville: Thomas Nelson, 1999), 44.
3. Gary Oliver, "Conflict: Friend or Foe?" Growthtrac, November 27, 2003, https://www.growthtrac.com/conflict-friend-or-foe/.
4. Greg Smalley, *Fight Your Way to a Better Marriage: How Healthy Conflict Can Take You to Deeper Levels of Intimacy* (New York: Howard Books, 2012), 9.

LIE #7: I'M GONNA MAKE YOU LOVE ME
1. The Jayhawks, "I'm Gonna Make You Love Me," track 2, *Smile*, Columbia, 2000, https://genius.com/the-jayhawks-im-gonna-make-you-love-me-lyrics.

LIE #9: YOU WIN SOME, YOU LOSE SOME
1. Mary J. Blige, "Kiss and Make Up," track 6, *Think Like a Man Too*, 2014, http://genius.com/mary-j-blige-kiss-and-make-up-lyrics.
2. Katy Perry, "Hot N Cold," track 7, *One of the Boys*, 2008, http://genius.com/katy-perry-hot-n-cold-lyrics.
3. Olga Khazan, "Nearly Half of All Murdered Women Are Killed by Romantic Partners," *The Atlantic*, July 20, 2017, https://www.theatlantic.com/health/archive/2017/07/homicides-women/534306/.
4. US Department of Justice, "Family Violence Statistics," June 2005, https://www.bjs.gov/content/pub/pdf/fvs03.pdf.

CONCLUSION: PUTTING IT ALL TOGETHER
1. Francis and Lisa Chan, *You and Me Forever: Marriage in Light of Eternity* (San Francisco: Claire Love Publishing, 2014).
2. Bill Moyer, "The Movement Action Plan: A Strategic Framework Describing the Eight Stages of Successful Social Movements," History Is a Weapon, spring 1987, http://www.historyisaweapon.com/defcon1/moyermap.html; Kevin Zeese and Margaret Flowers, "History Teaches That We Have the Power to Transform the Nation, Here's How," June 12, 2013, PopularResistance.org, https://popularresistance.org/history-teaches-that-we-have-the-power-to-transform-the-nation-heres-how/; Erica Chenoweth and Maria J. Stephan, *Why Civil Resistance Works: The Strategic Logic of Nonviolent Conflict* (New York: Columbia University Press, 2011).

More Resources to Help You Thrive in Marriage and Life

Starting now, this could be your best day, week, month, or year! Discover ways to express your needs, embrace your purpose, and love more fully. We offer life-transforming books, e-books, videos, devotionals, study guides, audiobooks, and audio dramas to equip you for God's calling on your life. Visit your favorite retailer, or go to **FocusOnTheFamily.com/resources**.

HOPE RESTORED®
A Marriage Intensive Experience

Where can I turn?
Who can I trust?
Why did this happen?

Questions race through your mind when your marriage is in crisis and the hurt runs deep. But there's still hope!

Your life and your marriage can be rebuilt at **Hope Restored®** a personalized, faith-based program for couples at the breaking point. Our unique clinical method, developed over 30 years by expert Christian counselors, has helped thousands of marriages with situations as messy and painful as yours.

* **Stop the Reactive Cycle** – Pinpoint what stokes your fears and anger when you face conflict and tension.
* **The Importance of Self-Care** – Learn what makes you healthy and whole, so you and your spouse can care for each other.
* **Distinguish between Oneness vs. Sameness** – Emotional connection starts with you. Then your spouse.

*Call us today for a FREE consultation and discover if **Hope Restored®** is right for you.*
HopeRestored.com or call 866-875-2915.

Since 2003...
7,000+ Couples in Crisis have found **hope**.

FOCUS ON THE FAMILY®

CP1588